College Writing

HOUGHTON MIFFLIN
ENGLISH FOR ACADEMIC SUCCESS

Karen E. Walsh

Northern Virginia Community College

SERIES EDITORS

Patricia Byrd

Joy M. Reid

Cynthia M. Schuemann

Houghton Mifflin Company

Boston   New York

Publisher: Patricia A. Coryell
Director of ESL Publishing: Susan Maguire
Senior Development Editor: Kathy Sands Boehmer
Developmental Editor: Lisa Weiner
Editorial Assistant: Evangeline Bermas
Senior Project Editor: Kathryn Dinovo
Manufacturing Assistant: Karmen Chong
Senior Marketing Manager: Annamarie Rice

Cover graphics: LMA Communications, Natick, Massachusetts

Photo credits: © Bettmann/Corbis, p. 2; © Royalty-Free/Corbis, p. 40; © Najlah Feanny/ Corbis, p. 40; © Jon Feingersh/Corbis, p. 78; © Larry Williams/Corbis, p. 130; © Larry Williams/Corbis, left, center, p. 130; ©LWA-Dann Tardif/Corbis, right, p.130; © Tom Stewart/Corbis, p. 188

Text credits: Reprinted by permission of the author, Kate Kinsella. From *Learning Styles in the ESL/EFL Classroom*, published by Heinle & Heinle, pp. 221–225. Copyright © 1993 by Kate Kinsella, p. 232.

Printed in the U.S.A.

Library of Congress Control Number: 2004112193

ISBN: 0-618-23028-9

23456789-CRW-08 07 06 05

Contents

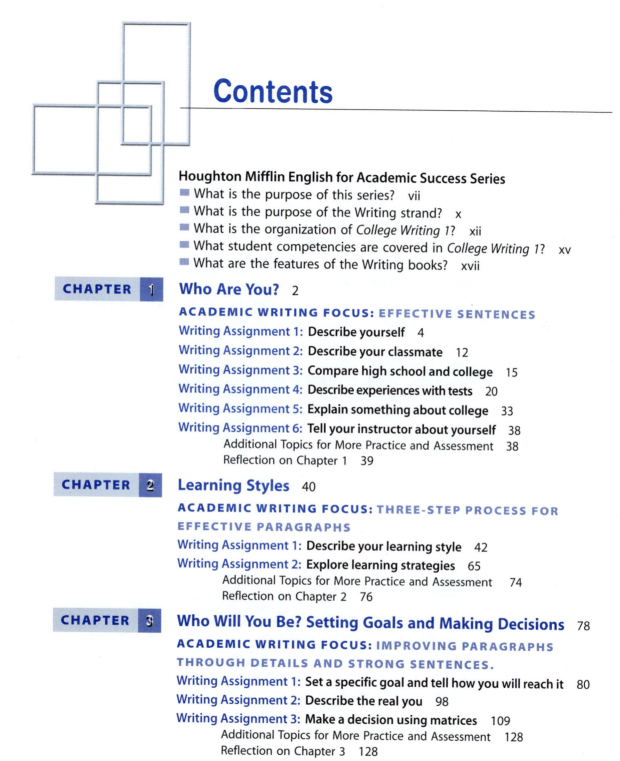

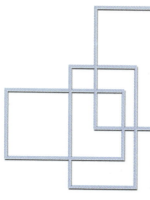

Houghton Mifflin English for Academic Success Series

SERIES EDITORS

Patricia Byrd, Joy M. Reid, Cynthia M. Schuemann

What Is the Purpose of This Series?

The Houghton Mifflin English for Academic Success series is a comprehensive program of student and instructor materials: four levels of student language proficiency textbooks in three skill areas (oral communication, reading, and writing) with supplemental vocabulary textbooks at each level. For instructors and students, a useful website supports classroom teaching, learning, and assessment. For instructors, four Essentials of Teaching Academic Language books (*Essentials of Teaching Academic Oral Communication, Essentials of Teaching Academic Reading, Essentials of Teaching Academic Writing,* and *Essentials of Teaching Academic Vocabulary*) provide helpful information for instructors new to teaching oral communication, reading, writing, and vocabulary.

The fundamental purpose of the series is to prepare students who are not native speakers of English for academic success in U.S. college degree programs. By studying these materials, students in college English for Academic Purposes (EAP) courses will gain the academic language skills they need to be successful students in degree programs. Additionally, students will learn about being successful students in U.S. college courses.

The series is based on considerable prior research as well as our own investigations of students' needs and interests, instructors' needs and desires, and institutional expectations and requirements. For example, our survey research revealed what problems instructors feel they face in their classrooms and what they actually teach; who the students are and what they know and do not know about the "culture" of U.S. colleges; and what types of exams are required for admission at various colleges.

Student Audience

The materials in this series are for college-bound ESL students at U.S. community colleges and undergraduate programs at other institutions. Some of these students are U.S. high school graduates. Some of them are long-term U.S. residents who graduated from a high school before coming to the United States. Others are newer U.S. residents. Still others are more typical international students. All of them need to develop academic language skills and knowledge of ways to be successful in U.S. college degree courses.

All of the books in this series have been created to implement the Houghton Mifflin English for Academic Success competencies. These competencies are based on those developed by ESL instructors and administrators in Florida, California, and Connecticut to be the underlying structure for EAP courses at colleges in those states. These widely respected competencies assure that the materials meet the real world needs of EAP students and instructors.

All of the books focus on . . .

- Starting where the students are, building on their strengths and prior knowledge (which is considerable, if not always academically relevant), and helping students self-identify needs and plans to strengthen academic language skills
- Academic English, including development of Academic Vocabulary and grammar required by students for academic speaking/listening, reading, and writing
- Master Student Skills, including learning style analysis, strategy training, and learning about the "culture" of U.S. colleges, which lead to their becoming successful students in degree courses and degree programs
- Topics and readings that represent a variety of academic disciplinary areas so that students learn about the language and content of the social sciences, the hard sciences, education, and business as well as the humanities

All of the books provide . . .

- Interesting and valuable content that helps the students develop their knowledge of academic content as well as their language skills and student skills
- A wide variety of practical classroom-tested activities that are easy to teach and engage the students
- Assessment tools at the end of each chapter so that instructors have easy-to-implement ways to assess student learning and students have opportunities to assess their own growth

- Websites for the students and for the instructors: the student sites will provide additional opportunities to practice reading, writing, listening, vocabulary development, and grammar. The instructor sites will provide instructor's manuals, teaching notes and answer keys, value-added materials like handouts and overheads that can be reproduced to use in class, and assessment tools such as additional tests to use beyond the assessment materials in each book.

What Is the Purpose of the Writing Strand?

The Writing strand of the Houghton Mifflin English for Academic Success series prepares ESL students for academic written work, particularly in the first two years of college study. Many ESL students have learned English mostly through their ears; others have studied English primarily with their eyes. Each group has unique written-language problems. The goals of the writing books are to build on the strengths of the students, to respect the knowledge they have, and to identify and teach language, content, and rhetoric that students must have to succeed in college courses. The writing strategies presented focus on confidence building and step-by-step, easy-to-learn processes for effective academic writing.

The four writing textbooks prepare students for the range of writing tasks assigned in college courses, and the solid scaffolding of skills focus on "college culture" as well as on academic writing. The high-interest content-based chapters relate to academic work and college disciplines, and the chapter materials have been designed to appeal to a variety of student learning styles and strategies. The authentic native-English speaker (NES), ESL, and professional writing samples offer students examples of required writing in post-secondary institutions; the writing assignments have been drawn from actual college courses across the curriculum. In addition, the content of each textbook is based on the Houghton Mifflin Writing Competencies, which in turn are based on state-designed competencies developed by hundreds of experienced ESL teachers.

Grammar and technology in the Writing strand

Because the ESL population is so diverse in its grammar and rhetoric needs, each chapter contains Power Grammar boxes that introduce structures needed by the students to write fluent, accurate academic prose. The structures are drawn from the writing required by the chapter content. Students who need additional work with the structures are referred to the Houghton Mifflin website, where high-quality relevant additional support is available.

Assignments in the writing textbooks also ask students to use the Internet: to investigate topics and to identify and evaluate sources for research. Materials about citing sources is sequenced and spiraled through the books so that students exit the writing program with substantial practice with and knowledge about using sources.

Assessment Materials Accompanying the Writing Strand

This Writing strand is filled with informal and formal assessment. Students write, self-assess, and have significant opportunities for peer response and other external informal review, including teacher response. The end of each chapter contains additional writing tasks for practice or for testing/evaluation. Each chapter also asks students to self-evaluate the skills they have learned; these self-evaluations have proven surprisingly honest and accurate, and the results allow teachers to review and recycle necessary concepts. Finally, students regularly return to the revision process, revising even their "final" drafts after the papers are returned by the teacher, and receiving grades for those revisions.

More formally, the instructor website (http://esl.college.hmco.com/instructors) and the *Essentials of Teaching Academic Writing* book offer assessment information and advice about both responding to and "grading" student writing. Information in these sources help instructors set up valid, reliable criteria for each student writing assignment in each book (which the instructors are encouraged to share with their students). These resources also contain sample student papers with teacher responses; sample topics to assess student strengths and weaknesses and to measure achievement and progress; and "benchmarked" student papers that describe the range of student grades.

Instructor Support Materials

The co-editors and Houghton Mifflin are committed to support instructors. For the Writing strand, the *Essentials of Teaching Academic Writing* by Joy Reid is an easily accessible, concise volume. This teacher resource, with its practical, problem-solving content, includes organizational suggestions for less experienced writing instructors, materials for response to and evaluation of student writing, and activities for teaching. In addition, each textbook has a password-protected website for instructors to provide classroom activities, substantial information and materials for assessment of student writing, and a "workbook" of printable pages linked to the textbook for use as handouts or overhead transparencies.

⬚ What Is the Organization of *College Writing 1*?

College Writing 1 prepares low-intermediate students for academic writing in U.S. colleges. The book teaches the basic elements of writing effective paragraphs. Students review English sentence structure and learn to write paragraphs for various purposes. The paragraphs may have as their purpose to describe, to persuade, to analyze or reflect, or a combination of these. Students learn a three-step writing process: Gathering Information, Focusing and Organizing, and Writing, Editing, and Revising. Short grammar teaching points are integrated into the writing process rather than taught for their own sake. Because many students at this level are new to the U.S. college experience, each chapter has a theme and writing topics that will contribute to the student's familiarity with academic culture. Chapter 1 focuses on comparing high school and college experiences. Chapter 2 topics revolve around learning styles and study strategies. The theme of Chapter 3 is setting goals and making decisions. Chapter 4 focuses on balancing the responsibilities of college study, family, and finances. Chapter 5 is about the student's experience with technology.

Chapter Organization

Each chapter has two to six writing assignments, in which the student is guided through a three-step writing process. The following common features appear in each chapter and support the writing process.

Spotlight on Writing Skills

Short explanations draw the student's attention to particular writing points that will be emphasized in the writing assignment and apply to successful academic writing.

Power Grammar

Each chapter provides a quick review or teaching point that allows students to self evaluate and instructors to determine if additional work is necessary. Two to four grammar points are presented, based on and integrated into the writing assignments.

Web Power

Web Power is a feature that reminds students that additional resources for practice of grammar points are provided on line.

Vocabulary Focus

Students add to a Word Bank of academic and other useful terms for each chapter. An asterisk in the text indicates that the word or term is a valuable one for academic writing. Word Bank forms are in the appendix, perforated for easy removal and use.

Graphic Organizers

Students learn to use graphic organizers to aid in writing and critical thinking.

Self-Editing and Peer Review

All writing assignments include self-editing and peer review exercises, using peer review sheets from the appendix.

Sample Paragraphs

Each chapter contains student writing samples for comparison, analysis, and discussion. Often, second drafts show how editing or revising improved a paragraph.

Reflection, Self-Evaluation, and Teacher Assessment of Student Writing

Each chapter ends with additional topics for practice and assessment, as well as reflection activities, giving students and the teacher an opportunity to assess mastery of key points taught in the chapter.

Acknowledgments

Many people contributed to the development of this book with their ideas and encouragement.

I would like to thank my editors at Houghton Mifflin, Susan Maguire and Kathy Sands Boehmer, for their help throughout the process of writing this series. Special thanks goes to the series editors, Joy Reid, Cynthia Schuemann, and Pat Byrd, for their unfailing enthusiasm, knowledge, and guidance throughout the process.

Faculty advisors who gave me advice and ideas are Linda Daubin, Mary Charleza, Carol Auerbach, Lisa Weiner, and Erica Berson.

The following reviewers contributed practical comments that shaped the revisions:

Amy Castrillon, Miami Dade Community College
Linda Choi, Canada College
Katherine Crawford, American River College
Shay Crawley, Mississippi State University
Virginia Edwards, Chandler-Gilbert Community College
Priscilla Eng, Middlesex Community College
David Kehe, Whatcom Community College
Elena Koulidoborova, Penn Valley Community College
Diane Kraemer, Hillsborough Community College
Barbara Sarapato, LaGuardia Community College and Columbia University
Judith Marasco, Santa Monica College
Maria Marin, DeAnza College
Carol Miele, Bergen Community College
Nancy Motz, CSU Fullerton
Patricia Plasket, Palm Beach Community College
Esther Robbins, Prince George's Community College
Anne-Marie Schlender, Austin Community College
Jenifer Taylor Cametti, Massasoit Community College
Elizabeth Wagenheim, Prince George's Community College.

Finally, I want to thank the many students who inspired me, especially those who permitted me to use their writing in this book: Abdel Albakhouchi, Labiba Wasiq, Shewit Gebrehiwot, Kenaane Mussie, Victor Flores, Ijaz Khalid, Karim Maaiez, Ana Moya, Marcella Castillo, Sung Shic Lee, Robel Romodan, Sedigheh Najafi, Yahya Ghobar, Javier Cortez, Waheeda Taheri, Sylvie Shabani, Nawal Mohamed, Tram Ly, Ghazala Kanwal, Angel Rivera, Kwaku Addo-Baffour, Ahmad Zubair Shorish, and Sohelee Haque Ditu.

▭ What Student Competencies Are Covered in *College Writing 1*?

Houghton Mifflin English for Academic Success Competencies

College Writing 1

Description of Overall Purposes

Students review basic English sentences structures and develop the ability to write accurate, fluent, multiple sentences about basic academic topics with an emphasis on the use of specific detail and sentence combining.

Materials in this textbook are designed with the following minimum exit objectives in mind:

Competency 1: (level/global focus) The student will compose texts appropriate to the level on experiential (descriptive and analytic) familiar academic topics with emphasis on use of specific detail.

Competency 2: (organization) The student will distinguish between general and specific (i.e. supporting) ideas, and to produce those details.

Competency 3: (grammar) The student will write accurate Standard English appropriate to the level.

Competency 4: (grammar) The student will practice proofreading and editing grammar and sentence structure appropriate to the level.

Competency 5: (vocabulary) The student will develop strategies for expanding academic vocabulary and using it in their writing.

Competency 6: (purpose) The student will develop proficiency on the Internet for academic purposes: to gather materials to support ideas.

Competency 7: (critical thinking) The student will develop the following critical thinking skills when writing:
A. identifying and analyzing audiences for their writing;
B. selecting appropriate detail; recognize the links between academic reading and writing; apply content knowledge to academic tasks (e.g., test-taking, reading and analyzing material in textbooks, analyzing Internet materials).

Competency 8:
(culture)
The student will recognize and discuss limited academic cultural references.

Competency 9:
(study strategies)
The student will enhance English/English dictionary and grammar reference skills.

Competency 10:
(study strategies)
The student will develop an awareness of study skills, learning styles, and strategies necessary when writing for academic purposes.

What Are the Features of the Writing Books?

The Houghton Mifflin English for Academic Success series is a comprehensive program of student and instructor materials. The fundamental purpose of the program is to prepare students who are not native speakers of English for academic success in U.S. college degree programs.

The Writing strand of the Houghton Mifflin English for Academic Success series focuses on the development of writing skills and general background knowledge necessary for college study. It is dedicated to meeting academic needs of students by teaching them how to handle the writing demands and expectations of college-level classes. The goals of the writing books are to build on the strengths of the students, to respect the knowledge they have, and to identify and teach language, content, and rhetoric that students must have to succeed in college courses.

Academic Content: The content of each book relates to academic subjects and has been selected because of its high interest for students and because of the popularity of these particular disciplines / courses on college campuses.

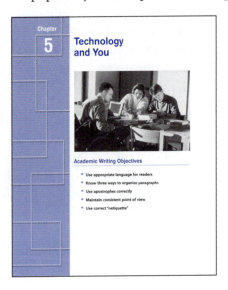

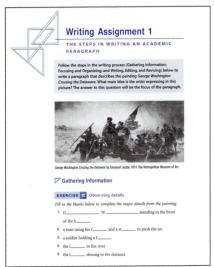

Authentic Writing Assignments: The writing assignments have been drawn from actual college courses across the curriculum. Students will find the assignments highly motivating when they realize they may receive such an assignment in one of their future classes.

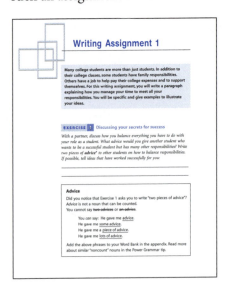

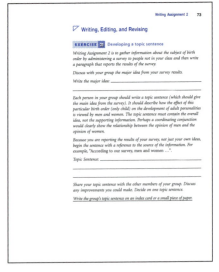

Authentic Writing Models: Models provide specific examples of student writing so that students can get compare writing styles, discuss writing strategies and understand instructor expectations.

Step-by-Step Writing Process: The step-by-step writing process helps demystify the concept of "academic writing" and helps students develop confidence. The textbooks offer solid scaffolding of skills that focus on college culture as well as on academic topics and academic writing. These are supplemented by practical advice offered in the Spotlight on Writing Skills feature boxes.

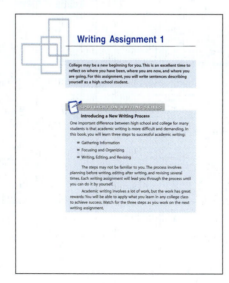

Self-Assessment Opportunity: A writing course develops through assessment. Students write and revise and instructors respond and evaluate and then students write some more. The textbooks offer students opportunity for peer review, self review, and self-evaluation.

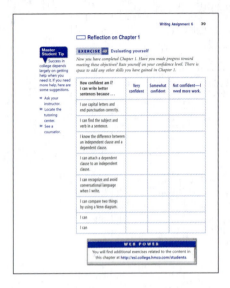

Master Student Tips: Master Student Tips throughout the textbooks provide students with short comments on a particular strategy, activity, or practical advice to follow in an academic setting.

Power Grammar Boxes: Students can be very diverse in their grammar and rhetorical needs so each chapter contains Power Grammar boxes that introduce the grammar structures students need to be fluent and accurate in academic English.

Ancillary Program: The ancillary program provides instructors with teaching tips, additional exercises, and robust assessment. Students can also take advantage of additional exercises and activities. The following items are available to accompany the Houghton Mifflin English for Academic Success series Writing strand.

- Instructor Website: Additional teaching materials, activities, and robust student assessment.
- Student Website: Additional exercises, activities, and web links.
- The Houghton Mifflin English for Academic Success series Vocabulary books: You can choose the appropriate level to shrinkwrap with your text.
- The *Essentials of Teaching Academic Writing* by Joy M. Reid is available for purchase. It gives you theoretical and practical information for teaching oral communication.

Who Are You?

Academic Writing Objectives

- Learn a three-step writing process

- Review sentence basics

- Write complete sentences

- Choose academic language

- Use enough details in descriptive writing

Here is what to expect in this chapter:

You will —write— sentences to	For the —purpose— of	Focus on —these— writing skills	Learn this —Power— Grammar	Use these —graphic— organizers	With this —vocabulary— focus
Describe yourself and your classmate Describe a classmate	Description	Learn a three-step writing process Write complete sentences Edit your work Use enough details Choose academic words	Sentence basics (capitalization & punctuation)	Matrix	Conversational vs. academic language
Compare high school and college	Comparison	Locate the subject and verb	Complete sentences—subject and verb	Venn diagram	Introduction to the Word Bank
Tell what you think about academic testing	Description	Use details Rewrite long sentences	Complete sentences—attach dependent to independent clauses		
Write a letter explaining something you have learned	Explanation Description	Choose academic words		Letter format Checklist	Choose academic language
Describe yourself to your instructor	Description Self-evaluation	Choose appropriate language		Letter format	Choose academic language

Writing Assignment 1

College may be a new beginning for you. This is an excellent time to reflect on where you have been, where you are now, and where you are going. For this assignment, you will write sentences describing yourself as a high school student.

 SPOTLIGHT ON WRITING SKILLS

Introducing a New Writing Process

One important difference between high school and college for many students is that academic writing is more difficult and demanding. In this book, you will learn three steps to successful academic writing:

- Gathering Information
- Focusing and Organizing
- Writing, Editing, and Revising

The steps may not be familiar to you. The process involves planning before writing, editing after writing, and revising several times. Each writing assignment will lead you through the process until you can do it by yourself.

Academic writing involves a lot of work, but the work has great rewards: You will be able to apply what you learn in any college class to achieve success. Watch for the three steps as you work on the next writing assignment.

▭ Gathering Information

Discussing who you were in high school

With one or two classmates, discuss your answers to these questions: As a high school student, who were you? What were you like?

- Were you a star student, a so-so student, or just an attendee?
- How hard did you try, and how much did you study?
- Socially, were you very popular, a loner, too busy to socialize, really shy, a nerd?
- Which crowd did you hang around with? People who spoke your first language, athletes, or the serious students?
- What was most important to you? Family, friends, people you worked with?
- How would you describe your high school experience? The best years of your life, the worst years of your life, or somewhere in between?

▭ Focusing and Organizing

EXERCISE 2 **Noticing the levels of language**

*While you were answering the questions in Exercise 1, did you notice the **conversational** or **informal** language? Can you think of **academic** or **formal** words that have the same meaning? The first one has been completed for you.*

Conversational language	Academic language
a star student	*an excellent student*
a so-so student	
a nerd	
hang around with	

SPOTLIGHT ON WRITING SKILLS

Conversational Language

Conversational language is appropriate for talking with people, but academic language is better for college writing.

- You might *say*, "I was a real nerd in high school."
  You might *write*, "In high school I was shy and not very popular."
- You might *say*, "I only hung out with people who spoke Spanish."
  You might *write*, "In high school, I preferred to be friends with other students who spoke Spanish."
- You might *say*, "My math teacher, Mrs. Smith, was awesome."
  You might *write*, "Mrs. Smith, my favorite math teacher, was an excellent instructor."

EXERCISE 3   **Describing yourself**

*Fill in the boxes with words that describe you in high school. Write as many words as you can for each level of language (**conversational** and **academic**), using the dictionary if you wish. A few examples have been added for you. Be sure to think about the differences between speaking and writing.*

	Descriptive words	
	Conversational	Academic
What were you like as a student?	(Examples: nerdy, a mess, a geek, teacher's pet)	(Examples: hard working, lazy, confused, enthusiastic, always eager to meet the teacher's expectations)
What was your attitude toward homework?		
How did you feel about tests and quizzes?		
How much did you participate in clubs and activities?		
How important were athletics to you?		
How important were grades to you?		
What were your friends like?	(Example: cool)	
If you had a job, what effect did it have on your education?		
Describe your relationships with teachers.	(Example: best buddies)	(Example: friendly)
Describe your relationships with counselors.		
How much pressure did you feel to do well?		

▭ Writing, Editing, and Revising

EXERCISE 4   Writing sentences about yourself

Write ten sentences describing yourself in high school. Use any of the descriptive words you wrote for Exercise 3.

1. _____

   _____

2. _____

   _____

3. _____

   _____

4. _____

   _____

5. _____

   _____

6. _____

   _____

7. _____

   _____

8. _____

   _____

9. _____

   _____

10. _____

   _____

*Circle all the **conversational words** you used in the ten sentences. How many are there? Write the number in this space: _____*

*Underline all the **academic words** you used in the ten sentences. How many are there? Write the number in this space: _____*

Based on your count, what do you think about your vocabulary?

_____ I am more comfortable with conversational words.

_____ I prefer academic words.

_____ I am comfortable with either level of vocabulary.

_____ I cannot tell the difference between conversational and academic words. I need more work.

WEB POWER

If you checked the last answer, use the Houghton Mifflin website **http://esl.college.hmco.com/students** for more work on word choices.

POWER GRAMMAR

Sentence Basics

In academic writing, your sentences must *look* like sentences.

All sentences start with a capital letter. Be sure you know the difference between **CAPITAL** and **lowercase** letters when you write.

INCORRECT: **m**y friends were not good students.
CORRECT: **M**y friends were not good students.

All sentences have punctuation at the end. Usually it is a period (.), a question mark (?), or an exclamation point (!).

I always had my homework ready**.** Why was I wasting my time**?** I loved high school**!**

EXERCISE **5**   **Checking your sentences**

Look at the ten sentences you wrote for Exercise 4. Check each for capitalization and end punctuation. Answer these questions:

- Does each sentence begin with a capital letter?   ____ Yes   ____ No
- Does each sentence end with a period, question mark, or exclamation point?   ____ Yes   ____ No

SPOTLIGHT ON WRITING SKILLS

Editing Your Work

In Exercise 5, you were asked to check each sentence for capitalization and punctuation. Another way to say this is *edit** **your work**. In writing, this means to check for mistakes. This is a very important skill to learn. In Appendix 1, you will find a Word Bank (p. 227). Use it to write words you find marked by the asterisk (*), such as *edit*. You may add other words you find in each chapter to your Word Bank to build your academic vocabulary.

EXERCISE **6**   **Reviewing your work with a peer**

Now give your sentences to a classmate. Ask your partner if your capital letters and end punctuation are clear. Answer the same questions for your partner's sentences.

How did you do?   _____ Great!   _____ I need more work.

WEB POWER

If you need more work, go to the Houghton Mifflin website **http://esl.college.hmco.com/students** for more exercises on sentence punctuation.

SPOTLIGHT ON WRITING SKILLS

Using Peer Reviews

Your classmates are your *peers*,* persons who have equal standing with you. Everyone benefits when you exchange writing and offer each other advice. If you are uncomfortable showing your work to another student or making comments on someone else's work, don't worry. You will soon see the advantages of peer review.

When you and your partner(s) review each other's work, keep in mind a few helpful hints:

- It is OK and even helpful to politely tell your partner if she needs to make some changes to her writing. Telling your partner everything is just fine will not help her improve her writing.
- Don't just say, "Your paragraph is good." Say, "I like your topic sentence because it is clear and specific." Be detailed in your feedback.
- Be nice. No one wants to hear, "Your paragraph is terrible. I can't understand half of what you are trying to say because your spelling is so bad." Instead, you can say, "I think that looking up the spelling of many of your words would help improve your paragraph."

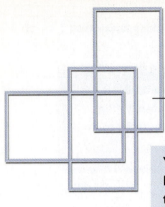

Writing Assignment 2

Your assignment is to write sentences about your partner from Exercise 6. You will use the sentences to introduce your partner to the class.

▭ Gathering Information

Use some of the sentences about your partner's high school experience. Try to give a complete picture of this person in high school.

EXERCISE 7 **Getting more details about your partner**

You may need to get more information from your partner to explain some of the sentences. For example, fill in the missing information blanks in this table to show which questions were asked and which answers were given. The first line (1) has been completed for you.

	He wrote	You ask	He adds	You write (for example)
1	I played on several teams.	Which sports?	soccer, tennis, and basketball	He played on the soccer, tennis, and basketball teams.
2	I hated my classes.		I was bored and didn't want to be in ESL.	He hated his classes because he was bored and didn't want to be in ESL.
3	My grades **stunk**.	How bad were they?		His grades were so bad that he had to go to summer school before his senior year.

Did you notice that some words were changed from informal language to more appropriate language? Academic language is always more appropriate in the classroom, even for an oral presentation. For example, if your partner wrote, "My grades **stunk**," you would write (and say), "His grades were **so bad** . . ."

EXERCISE **8** **Writing sentences describing your partner**

Write five-to-ten sentences you will use to describe your partner.

1. _____

_____

2. _____

_____

3. _____

_____

4. _____

_____

5. _____

_____

6. _____

_____

7. _____

_____

8. _____

_____

9. _____

_____

10. _____

_____

EXERCISE 9 Editing your sentences

Now look at each sentence and circle the answer:

Yes   No   Each sentence begins with a capital letter.

Yes   No   Each sentence ends with a period, question mark, or
            exclamation point.

Yes   No   I used academic (formal) language in each sentence.

Yes   No   I used enough descriptive words to give a picture of
            my partner.

*If you cannot answer yes to each question, go back and work on your
sentences until you can. Practice reading the sentences to your partner.
Then introduce your partner to the class by reading the sentences aloud.*

Writing Assignment 3

In this assignment, you will compare high school and college. (Your high school experience could be either in the United States or in another country.) Is college what you expected it to be, so far? Are you surprised or even shocked by the differences between your expectations and reality? Are high school and college similar or different, in your experience?

▭ Gathering Information

SPOTLIGHT ON WRITING SKILLS

Using Venn Diagrams to Gather and Organize Information

*Venn diagrams** are a great way to organize your thoughts. You can use them to compare any two or more things and identify the similarities and differences. A Venn diagram uses overlapping circles to represent groups of ideas or objects. In the overlapping part are similarities between the things. In the parts of the circles that do not intersect are differences. If this is the first time you have seen this term, add it to your vocabulary. You will find it a useful phrase to know in college and may use it in other classes, such as mathematics.

EXERCISE 10 **Making a Venn diagram**

Complete the Venn diagram to compare high school and college. Consider the amount of reading, the size of the classes, the teachers, the time spent studying, and other things you have noticed.

- In the left circle, write words or phrases that describe high school but not college.
- In the right circle, write words or phrases that describe college but not high school.
- In the center, where the circles intersect, write words or phrases that describe both high school and college.

High School   **Both**   **College**

Time to socialize   Lots of new friends   Harder reading

▢ Focusing and Organizing

EXERCISE 11 **Comparing your diagrams**

When you have written as many words and phrases as you can in your Venn diagram, compare your ideas with those of three classmates. Are your Venn diagrams about the same, or are they different?

Remember that the words may be a little different, but their meanings may still be similar. For example, "time to socialize" and "I spent all my evenings and weekends hanging out with my friends" are common ideas.

▢ Writing, Editing, and Revising

EXERCISE 12 **Writing your sentences**

On the next page, list any ideas you had in common. Write each idea as a complete sentence.

	(Write as complete sentences)
We agreed on these ideas about high school:	
We agreed on these ideas about college:	
We agreed that college and high school are _similar_ in these ways:	

EXERCISE 13   **Reviewing what you know**

How do you know whether your sentences are complete? Study the Power Grammar before you check your sentences.

POWER GRAMMAR

Complete Sentences—Part 1

When you write, your sentences must be complete. Incomplete sentences are used in speaking but should be avoided in academic writing.

To be complete, a sentence must have a subject and a verb. The subject usually comes first in a sentence.	subject College is more difficult than high school. 　　subject Our group had more fun in high school.
The verb often follows the subject in the sentence.	verb College is more difficult than high school. 　　　　verb Our group had more fun in high school.
There may be other words in a sentence, too, like an object.	Our group had more _fun_ in high school than in college.

EXERCISE 14   Locating subjects and verbs

In each of these sentences, draw one line under the subject and two lines under the verb.

Example: Our group had more fun in high school than in college.

1. Homework takes more time in college.

2. High school work wasn't very difficult for us.

3. Our teachers were friendlier in high school.

4. We pay tuition in college.

5. Both high school and college give choices on classes to take.

EXERCISE 15   Editing your group's sentences

With the same group for Exercise 11, check your group's sentences about the differences and similarities between high school and college.

- One member will underline subjects and verbs.

- The second member will check to be sure the first word in each sentence is capitalized.

- The third member will check the end punctuation.

- The fourth member will change any conversational language to academic language.

How did your group do?

_____ Great! We found all the subjects, verbs, and objects.

_____ Not so well, but we fixed the mistakes (we think).

_____ Help! We are lost. *(If you need help, ask your instructor.)*

EXERCISE 16 Writing your five most interesting sentences

Together, decide on the five most interesting sentences your group wrote.
Write them here:

1. _____

   _____

   _____

2. _____

   _____

   _____

3. _____

   _____

   _____

4. _____

   _____

   _____

5. _____

   _____

   _____

Your instructor will tell you whether you should turn in your work.

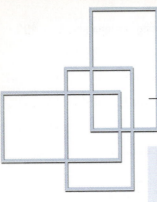

Writing Assignment 4

Tests, exams, and quizzes are an important part of high school and college life. How do you feel about them? For this writing assignment, you will describe your experience with and attitude toward tests.

▭ Gathering Information

EXERCISE 17 Checking how you feel about academic tests

Circle either True or False for each statement.

1. True   False   I welcome tests as a way to find out how much I know.

2. True   False   I look at tests as something I don't like but have to do.

3. True   False   I'm very competitive, so I love tests.

4. True   False   I know some techniques to help me do well on tests.

5. True   False   My heart races and my palms sweat before a test.

6. True   False   I don't do well on tests because I forget everything.

7. True   False   I always stay up all night before a test to study.

8. True   False   Tests aren't fair because teachers ask trick questions.

9. True   False   I could get better grades if I had more time on tests.

10. True   False   College tests are more difficult than high school tests.

EXERCISE 18 Discussing your answers

With another student, discuss your answers on Exercise 17. Are they similar or different?

EXERCISE 19 Reading student samples

Read what Abdel wrote about tests. Then answer the questions in Exercise 20.

Student Sample 1

> Since the age of seven I have had to take tests every semester and every end of year. So I can say that taking exams has become habitual for me. That doesn't mean I'm not afraid, but my reaction differs from exam to exam. In my opinion, being afraid of the test means that you care about it and you want to pass it. And this worry and fear will be just in the beginning. After you start the test, you forget everything, and you concentrate on what you are doing. My experience taught me if I don't want to be afraid in the exam or the test, first I have to review my lessons, do all my homework before taking a test, and start with what I know. Finally, I try to focus on my test so I don't waste my time. This is good advice for other students.
>
> Abdel

EXERCISE 20 Comprehending questions

Read the paragraph that Abdel wrote about his feelings before a test. Answer these questions about Abdel:

1. Abdel thinks that being afraid may actually be a good sign. What does he think the fear means? _____

2. What does he do to lessen his fear of tests? _____

Read what Labiba wrote about tests. Then answer the questions in Exercise 21.

Student Sample 2

Anxiety before a test is always there because I cannot predict anything about my test, and it makes me very thoughtful about what the exam or question will be like because the phase of anticipation is very hard, but at the time of the exam, every hidden idea is revealed and no more anxiety is left except for timing, so in order to control my anxiety, to be more confident and concentrate and not to think about anything else, I just relax and believe in myself. My advice to any student is to be prepared, study, and learn hard before a test and concentrate at the time of the test.

Labiba

EXERCISE 21   **Comprehending more questions**

Answer these questions about Labiba's advice:

1. Why does Labiba feel anxious before the test?

   _____

   _____

2. What is Labiba's advice to students?

   _____

   _____

3. How many words does Labiba's first sentence contain? The sentence is underlined.

   _____

   _____

When you were reading Labiba's writing, did you notice how long her first sentence is? Could you say it out loud in a single breath? Would you agree that her sentence is too long?

_____ Yes _____ No

Most people say that Labiba's first sentence is too long.

EXERCISE 22 **Analyzing a long sentence**

List the ideas in Labiba's first sentence separately. The first and second ideas have been completed for you. The connecting words have been put in brackets.

1. _Anxiety before a test is always there_ _____ [because]

2. _I cannot predict anything about my test,_ _____ [and]

3. _____ [because]

4. _____ [but]

5. _____ [and]

6. _____ [so]

7. _____ .

EXERCISE 23 **Rewriting Labiba's long sentence**

Divide Labiba's sentence into three or more shorter sentences.

_____

_____

_____

_____

_____

_____

_____

Read her new sentences aloud.

- Are they more comfortable to say?
- Do they sound appropriate?
- Do they reflect Labiba's ideas?
- Compare your revised sentences with a classmate's sentences.
    - How are the sentences similar?
    - In what ways are they different?

EXERCISE 24 **Checking the new sentences for completeness**

After you wrote new sentences for Labiba, did you:

- Check for a capital letter at the beginning of each sentence?
- Check for end punctuation?
- Check for a subject and verb for each sentence?

Even if you answered Yes for each question, your sentences may still have a completeness problem. Read this Power Grammar tip to find out why.

POWER GRAMMAR

Complete Sentences—Part 2

Incomplete sentences are sometimes caused by dependent clauses standing alone.

All clauses have a subject and a verb. (You already know this!)

subject   verb
When I study,

subject verb
I am not anxious before tests.

But having a subject and a verb is not enough. Often the problem is simply that a dependent clause is not connected to an independent clause.

Dependent clause: When I study

Independent clause: I am not anxious before tests.

The difference is that the *independent* clause can stand by itself—it sounds complete to the listener.

I am not anxious before tests.

A *dependent* clause often doesn't sound right by itself. People will want to ask more questions if they hear a dependent clause out of context. (That means completely on its own.)

When I study

(What do you mean? Finish your sentence!)

(Continued)

Dependent clauses begin with a word like **when**, **before**, **after**, **as soon as**, **although**, **if**, and **because**. These are the most common signals that the clause is *dependent* and must be attached to an *independent* clause.

dependent   independent

clause   clause

When I study, I am not anxious before tests.

(Notice the comma <u>after</u> the dependent clause.

Here is an easy way to remember that the dependent clause must be attached to an independent clause: think of the *dependent* clause as a *child* and the *independent* clause as the *parent*.

independent dependent	dependent independent
(father) (child)	(child) (mother)
I reward myself after I study.	After I study, I reward myself.

Parents don't let their children run around by themselves—they hold them by the hand. Think of the connecting words as hands—**when**, **before**, **after**, **as soon as**, **although**, **if**, **because**. These words link the parent to the child and keep the child safe.

If the *dependent* clause comes at the beginning of the sentence, you must put a comma after it. If the *independent* clause comes first, don't put a comma between it and the dependent clause.

dependent   independent

clause   clause

If I study, I usually pass tests.

independent   dependent

clause   clause

I usually pass tests if I study.

EXERCISE 25   **Attaching dependent clauses**

*Examples, of words that introduce dependent clauses are **when, before, after, because, as soon as, although,** and **if**. Make the following dependent clauses into complete sentences by adding an independent clause to each. The first one has been completed for you.*

1. **As soon as** I know about a test,

   _I make my study plan_____.

2. **Although** Abdel is afraid at the beginning of the test,

   _____.

3. **When** students study for tests,

   _____.

4. **After** Labiba relaxes,

   _____.

5. _____

   if you haven't studied enough.

6. _____

   as soon as the teacher announced the grades.

7. **When** you arrive in class with plenty of time before the test,

   _____.

8. **Because** I eat a big breakfast before a test,

   _____.

9. _____,

   although I thought I studied enough.

10. **As soon as** I finish the test,

   _____.

WEB POWER

You will find additional exercises related to the content in this chapter at http://esl.college.hmco.com/students.

⬜ Focusing and Organizing

EXERCISE 26 **Getting ready to write**

Discuss with another student your experiences taking tests and exams. Try to remember times that were typical.

⬜ Writing, Editing, and Revising

EXERCISE 27 **Writing your sentences**

Think about your discussion with another student. Then write at least five sentences describing your usual reaction to tests and exams. Be sure to describe your physical, emotional, and mental reactions in a test experience. Use words that describe how you feel. In at least two sentences, use some of these words: **when**, **before**, **as soon as**, **because**, **if**, **after**, *and* **although**.

Write your sentences here:

1. _____

   _____

2. _____

   _____

3. _____

   _____

4. _____

   _____

5. _____

   _____

6. _____

_____

7. _____

_____

8. _____

_____

9. _____

_____

10. _____

_____

EXERCISE **28**   **Checking your sentences for completeness**

Write the subject and the verb for each sentence.

Sentence number	Subject	Verb
1		
2		
3		
4		
5		
6		
7		
8		
9		
10		

EXERCISE 29 Checking for dependent clauses

Below, write the sentences containing these words: **when, before, after, as soon as, although, because,** *and* **if.**

1. _____

_____

2. _____

_____

3. _____

_____

4. _____

_____

5. _____

_____

Check each sentence to be sure you attached any dependent clause to an independent clause.

- Put brackets [ ] around each dependent clause.
- Draw a line under the connecting word.
- Put these curly brackets { } around the independent clause.

For example:

dependent clause   independent clause
[When *I take a test*], {I always start by reading the directions carefully}.

EXERCISE 30 Evaluating your writing

- Did you remember to add the comma if the dependent clause is before the independent clause?
- Did you begin each sentence with a capital letter and end it with punctuation?
- Did you put **brackets*** and **curly brackets*** in your Word Bank?
- After you have corrected any problems in your sentences, hand them in to your instructor.

Master Student Tip

Learning to relax is one important way to improve your performance on tests.

EXERCISE 31 Discussing your favorite relaxation technique

In a small group, talk with your classmates about your favorite relaxation techniques to use before or during tests. For example, you might discuss what you do the night before a test, the morning of a test, or just before a test. What do you do to relax your body? What do you do to relax your mind?

EXERCISE 32 Relaxing for success: Add the verbs

The sentences below describe a technique to relax before a test (adapted from *Becoming a Master Student,* Dave Ellis, 2003, p. 178).

Read it with a partner.

- Together, highlight the subject for each blank.

- Fill in the blanks with verbs from the box.

- Try to use each verb at least once.

- More than one verb may fit in some blanks.

- You may have to change the verb form to make it fit.

- Add any words you do not know to your Word Bank.

be (is/are/was/were)	close	discover	do	feel
hear	imagine	learn	move	release
see	sit	visualize	watch	know
have				

When Thomas _was_ a high school student, _he used/discovered/_ _learned_ a technique to help him control his fear of taking tests. It was called "Rehearsing for Success." He practiced this relaxation and visualization technique many times BEFORE taking a test.

This is how he _____ it. He _____ in a chair, legs and arms uncrossed. He _____ his eyes, letting go of all thoughts, and focused on his breathing for a minute or two.

Then he relaxed parts of his body, beginning with his feet. He _____ his toes and his ankles. He _____ up to his calves and thighs. He relaxed the muscles of his lower back, abdomen, and chest. Then he _____ all the tension in his hands, arms, shoulders, and finally his neck, jaw, eyelids, and scalp.

When Thomas _____ completely relaxed, he _____ himself in an exam room. It was the day of the test. He visualized himself taking the test successfully, and each detail of the experience became clear. He _____ the test being handed out. He noticed his surroundings. He _____ the other students shuffle in their seats. He _____ the desk, the pen in his hand, and the exam in front of him. He _____ himself looking over the exam calmly and confidently. He discovered that he _____ all the answers.

Then Thomas _____ himself writing quickly. He _____ himself turn in the test with confidence. Finally, he _____ receiving the test grade. It _____ an A. He savored the feeling.

EXERCISE 33 **Relaxing ideas to reduce anxiety**

Here are some more ideas from experts (including students) on how to reduce test anxiety and do better on tests. Check the ones you already use and the ones you would like to try:

Idea	I've tried this.	I would like to try this.
1. Plan your studying so that you have enough time before the test.		
2. Use tutoring and other help available at your college.		
3. Form a study group with other students in the same class.		
4. Repeat positive statements to boost your confidence ("I am really well prepared," "I can do this.")		
5. Study for several short periods of time rather than one long period of time.		
6. Get a good night's sleep before the test.		
7. Improve your note-taking skills.		
8. Arrive early for the test, with all the materials you will need.		
9. Try to predict test questions.		
10. Tell yourself a test is an opportunity to learn what you know, and you will use it to improve.		
11. Ask yourself what's the worst thing that will happen to you if you fail the test. (Usually, the answer is nothing terrible!)		

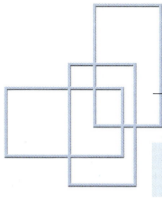

Writing Assignment 5

Write a letter to a person, based on the knowledge you now have that you didn't have in high school. Choose from this list.

- A letter to a student in your high school, telling him or her <u>something</u> important he or she needs to understand in order to be prepared for college.
- A letter to an instructor you had in high school, thanking the person for <u>something</u> you learned in her or his class that is helping you in college.
- A letter to your high school counselor, explaining <u>one thing</u> you needed to know (but didn't) in order to adjust to college.

Gathering Information

EXERCISE 34 **Making a list**

One way to plan before you write is to make a list of details you want to include to explain <u>the one thing</u> you want to say to the person.

For example, look at the letter Lisa wrote to her high school counselor. (See Exercise 36.) Answer these questions:

- What is the one thing she wants the counselor to know?

  _____

- What are some of the details she uses to explain to the counselor the importance of high school instructors being stricter about students' writing?

  _____

  _____

- What does she ask the counselor to tell the English instructors?

  _____

  _____

⬚ Focusing and Organizing

EXERCISE **35** **Planning your letter**

Now write the one important thing you want to say in your letter:

_____

_____

_____

_____

_____

_____

List the details you will use in the letter.

_____

_____

_____

_____

_____

_____

_____

_____

_____

_____

_____

▭ Writing, Editing, and Revising

EXERCISE 36 Writing your letter

Write your letter, using the format Lisa used.

January 20, 200__

(Note the comma after the name)

Dear Mrs. Henderson,

(Indent the first line of the body of the letter)

Thank you for being my counselor. Now that I am in college, I want to tell you what I have learned. It is that high school instructors should be stricter and make sure they give us feedback on what are mistakes in our writing. When instructors gave us homework, students just wrote down any answer. We knew they would check to see if we did it, but not if we did it right.

When I took the college placement test, I was shocked! I have to take ESL classes before I can take freshman English for credit. I didn't know my writing was so bad. Please ask the English instructors to warn the students so that they pass the placement test.

(Note the comma)

Sincerely,

Lisa N_____

Leave a 1-inch margin on the left

Leave a ½-inch margin on the right

EXERCISE 37   Reviewing your letter format

After you have completed your letter, check it carefully against the sample letter. Then answer these questions:

■ Is the date in the correct place?	____ Yes	____ No
■ Is the person's title used (Mr./Mrs./Ms.)?	____ Yes	____ No
■ Is there a comma after the name of the person?	____ Yes	____ No
■ Is each paragraph indented?	____ Yes	____ No
■ Is there an appropriate *closing** (Sincerely, Yours truly,)?	____ Yes	____ No
■ Are the margins correct?	____ Yes	____ No

EXERCISE 38   Editing your letter

Now check your letter for sentence correctness and language level.

First, highlight or underline each subject and verb.

Second, circle these words: when, before, after, as soon as, although, because, if.

Circle Yes or No for each question:

■ Does each clause have a subject and verb?	Yes	No
■ Is each dependent clause attached to an independent clause?	Yes	No
■ Does each sentence begin with a capital letter?	Yes	No
■ Does each sentence end with punctuation?	Yes	No
■ Did you use academic language (not conversational language)?	Yes	No

EXERCISE 39 Reviewing peers

Which assignment did you do?

- A letter to a **student** in your high school, telling the person something important he or she needs to understand in order to be prepared for college

- A letter to an **instructor** you had in high school, thanking the person for something you learned in her or his class that is helping you in college

- A letter to your high school **counselor**, explaining one thing you needed to know (but didn't) in order to adjust to college

Find someone in your class who did the same assignment. Exchange letters with your classmate. Read each other's letters:

- Tell your partner *one thing* about the letter you liked *the most*.

- Give your partner *one suggestion* on how to *improve* the letter.

After you have heard your classmate's ideas about your letter, decide whether you want to change anything. Then rewrite your letter and give it to your instructor.

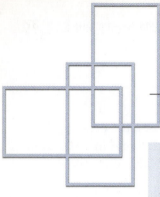

Writing Assignment 6

As a final writing assignment, follow the three-step process you have learned to write five to ten sentences telling your instructor about yourself as a college student. First, **gather** information. Then, **focus and organize** your ideas. Finally, **write**, **edit**, and **revise** your sentences.

You may want to write about some (but not all) of these issues:

- How have you changed since high school?
- What has surprised you about college?
- How is college writing different from high school writing (or similar to it)?
- What has been your greatest challenge as a college student, so far?
- What were your reasons for registering for classes at this college?
- What kind of college student would you like to be?

Additional Topics for More Practice and Assessment

Topics for Timed or Independent Writing

- Describe your favorite technique for relaxing before a test or during a test. Write at least five sentences. Use specific details so that the reader can understand the technique.
- Describe the most important thing you learned in high school. Why was it so important?
- Describe a new friend you have made since becoming a college student.
- Describe a positive or negative experience you had in high school that taught you a valuable lesson.
- Describe some advice someone gave you about college that has helped you.
- Draw a Venn diagram comparing yourself with the person you introduced to the class.

Reflection on Chapter 1

Master Student Tip

Success in college depends largely on getting help when you need it. If you need more help, here are some suggestions.

- Ask your instructor.
- Locate the tutoring center.
- See a counselor.

EXERCISE 40 **Evaluating yourself**

Now you have completed Chapter 1. Have you made progress toward meeting these objectives? Rate yourself on your confidence level. There is space to add any other skills you have gained in Chapter 1.

How confident am I? I can write better sentences because . . .	Very confident	Somewhat confident	Not confident—I need more work.
I use capital letters and end punctuation correctly.			
I can find the subject and verb in a sentence.			
I know the difference between an independent clause and a dependent clause.			
I can attach a dependent clause to an independent clause.			
I can recognize and avoid conversational language when I write.			
I can compare two things by using a Venn diagram.			
I can			
I can			

W E B   P O W E R

You will find additional exercises related to the content in this chapter at **http://esl.college.hmco.com/students**.

Learning Styles

Academic Writing Objectives

- Use the three-step process for writing a paragraph

- Check for subject-verb agreement

- Use the correct verb tense for the right meaning (present or past?)

Here is what to expect in this chapter:

You will write a paragraph on	For the purpose of	Focus on these writing skills	Learn this Power Grammar	Use these graphic organizers	With this vocabulary focus
Your learning style	Description	Use the three-step writing process for a paragraph Develop a topic sentence Focus ideas and details Write a concluding sentence Use academic format standards	Subject-verb agreement Use the right tense for the right meaning (present or past?)	Freewriting Peer review form Paragraph organization table	
Study strategies to suit your learning styles	Analysis	Use academic vocabulary		Learning style survey Study strategy plan Peer review form	Vocabulary for learning styles and strategies Ways to learn vocabulary Take a learning styles survey

Writing Assignment 1

Your first writing assignment is to describe your learning style preferences in a paragraph. The paragraph will be about seven to ten sentences long. You will be guided through the three steps of the writing process introduced in Chapter 1:

■ **Gathering Information**

■ **Focusing and Organizing**

■ **Writing, Editing, and Revising**

But before you begin, be sure you understand what you should do. Your writing must always respond to the assignment. If it does not, it will fail, no matter how well you wrote. So ask yourself questions first. If you do not know the answers, ask your instructor.

1. What am I going to write? (A sentence? A paragraph? An essay?)

2. Do I know what a paragraph is? (How long? How will it be organized? How will it look?)

3. Do I understand the topic? (What am I supposed to write about?)

4. Who is my audience? (Who will be reading this? What do they already know about me? What do they know about the topic?)

5. What is the purpose of the assignment? (To give my opinion? To prove a point? To explain something? To research the topic?)

6. How much time do I have to complete this assignment? (An hour? A day? A week?)

7. Whom can I talk with about this assignment? (My instructor? Other students? Tutors at the learning center?)

⬜ Gathering Information

EXERCISE 1 Thinking about how students learn

Think about these statements and whether they apply to you. With another student, discuss two or three statements that interest you.

- Some students like to learn by reading about a topic.
  Explain why this might be so.

- Some students prefer to learn by listening to a lecture.
  Is this you? Do you remember what you hear?

- Some choose to learn by doing.
  Describe a time when you learned how to do something by actually doing it.

- Some students like to learn alone.
  Does this appeal to you?

- Some learn better when they work with a partner or a small group.
  Does this describe you, or do you prefer learning alone?

- Successful students often have more than one learning style.
  Can you explain this statement?

- Most students can expand their learning styles with experimentation and practice.
  Have you ever experimented with learning something a different way from your usual approach?

EXERCISE **2** **Reading about learning styles**

Abdel and Shewit are in their first semester in a community college. They wrote about the importance of understanding how they learn. (You may notice some mistakes in their writing.) Read their paragraphs, and then answer the questions in Exercise 3.

Student Sample 1

I think that it's important to know about learning styles. First the person has to know his styles. What style is good for him? What does he like? After that he has to look for the other styles and try them. For me I like to work or to learn by myself, but I think that is not enough. Working with a group help too and sometimes it is much better. I think that the person has to know about all the styles and try to practice them because he will need them. Learning by listening is good but you have to read and learn by reading too. If you have just one way to learn, like working in a group, sometimes this group can't give anything because they wants to learn from you. In this case you have to practice another style.

Abdel

Student Sample 2

It is important to know what my learning method is, because sometimes some people are smart but when the teacher tell them to do something in different ways their knowledge disappear. They get confused and it is also good for your teachers that deals with you on a daily basis to understand how they can help you.

Shewit

EXERCISE 3 Checking your comprehension

Answer these questions about Abdel and Shewit.

1. How does Abdel prefer to study?

   _____

2. Does Shewit say what her preferred learning style is?

   _____

3. Why does Abdel think it is important to learn other styles?

   _____

4. Does Shewit think that teachers can help students more if they know the students' learning styles?

   _____

EXERCISE 4 Checking the verbs

Abdel and Shewit have made some grammar errors in their paragraphs. Fill in the boxes with your suggestions for how they should correct the verbs. Each verb problem is underlined. Then compare your answers with a classmate's.

Abdel's paragraph	
Abdel wrote	**Abdel should write it this way**
Working with a group <u>help</u> too . . .	Working with a group help<u>s</u> too . . .
. . . they <u>wants</u> to learn from you.	

Shewit's paragraph	
Shewit wrote	**Shewit should write it this way**
. . . but when the teacher <u>tell</u> them to do something . . .	. . . but when the teacher tell<u>s</u> them to do something . . .
. . . their knowledge <u>disappear</u>.	
. . . your teachers that <u>deals</u> with you	

Here are some tips to help you with verbs.

POWER GRAMMAR

Subject-Verb Agreement

To be an academic writer, you have to use the correct form of the verb to match the subject.

All sentences have a subject and a verb. If the subject is singular, then the verb must be singular.

singular singular
subject verb
The <u>book</u> <u>is</u> mine.

If the subject is plural, then the verb must be plural.

plural subject plural verb
The <u>books</u> <u>are</u> mine.

The subject agrees with the verb no matter how many words come between the subject and the verb. (Don't be fooled! The word next to the verb may *not* be the subject.)

singular subject
The <u>book</u> on the stack of
 singular verb
papers <u>is</u> mine.

plural subject
The <u>books</u> on the stack of
 plural verb
papers <u>are</u> mine.

Anyone, anybody, someone, somebody, everyone, everybody, anything, everything, and *something* all use singular verbs, although it may seem that they refer to several people or things.

singular verb
Anyone <u>is</u> welcome.

singular verb
Everyone <u>is</u> welcome.

Be careful with *noncount nouns.* They use singular verbs. (You will learn more about noncount nouns in Chapter 4.)

noncount subject singular verb
The <u>homework</u> <u>seems</u> difficult.

noncount subject singular verb
My <u>vocabulary</u> <u>grows</u> day
by day.

EXERCISE 5 **Testing your subject-verb agreement**

First, underline or highlight the subject for each verb choice. Then, choose the right verb.

Each day in his ESL class, John *feels / feel* a little more frustrated. He tries to be a good student. He never *arrives / arrive* late to class. He always *finishes / finish* his homework before class *begins / begin*, but he is worried because his test grades *is / are* low. Although he *studies / study* for at least two hours every night, he never *earns / earn* a grade higher than 65 percent.

John has noticed that he has trouble understanding the lessons that the instructors *presents / present*. They usually *lectures / lecture* from their desk at the front of the classroom. Most instructors *doesn't write / don't write* anything on the blackboard. Sometimes John *doesn't hear / don't hear* what Mr. Smith, his English instructor, is saying. Other times, John finds he cannot take good notes so that he can review the lesson after class. This is John's first semester at Alexandria Community College, and, like many other students, he is afraid to talk to the instructor. New students often *worries / worry* that an instructor will think they are stupid, so no one *wants / want* to say anything.

Each semester at midterm, everybody in the class *meets / meet* with Mr. Smith to talk about the midterm grade. Mr. Smith tells John his midterm grade is F and asks how he can help him. John is embarrassed, but he *suggests / suggest*, "I think I would do better if you wrote your notes on the board. I can't remember something if I don't see it written."

"Oh, I *understand / understands*," says Mr. Smith. "You are a visual learner. You learn by seeing. I'll use the overhead projector for the notes."

John feels very relieved. He *wishes / wish* he had told Mr. Smith about his problems at the beginning of the semester. After thinking about what the instructor said, John *understands / understand* that he really does learn better when he can see what he is supposed to learn.

EXERCISE **6** **Practicing subject-verb agreement**

Choose a verb for each blank. Underline or highlight the subject for the verb to help you decide whether to use the -s form. Verbs may be used more than once. Compare your answers with those of a classmate.

believe	get	learn	like	need
prefer	think	try	understand	work

1. A <u>student</u> who is a **tactile*** learner usually <u>*likes*</u> to use her or his senses. (I chose **likes** because the subject, *student*, is singular.)

2. Abdel often _____ to work by himself.

3. Now, however, when Abdel _____ in a group, he _____ to enjoy it.

4. He _____ that working by himself is not enough.

5. Shewit _____ that her teachers _____ to know her learning style so that they can help her.

6. John and many of his classmates _____ **visually.***

7. Now John _____ that he must ask the teacher for what he _____.

8. John always _____ hard, but he usually _____ low test scores.

9. **Kinesthetic*** learners _____ to participate in physical activities.

10. They _____ to move around when they are learning.

11. Each student _____ to determine her or his own learning style.

12. Everyone _____ in a special way.

Adding to Your Word Bank

When you see this symbol, *, the asterisk, you will know that this word may be important for college-level work. Remember to add it to your Word Bank in the appendix, just as you did in Chapter 1.

WEB POWER

Do you need more practice on subject-verb agreement? You will find additional exercises related to this content in this chapter at http://esl.college.hmco.com/students.

SPOTLIGHT ON WRITING SKILLS

Freewriting

*Freewriting** is a good way to gather your thoughts as you begin the assignment. To freewrite means to write quickly as much as you can on a topic. Do not worry about spelling, punctuation, or grammar. Just write any thought that comes to mind.

EXERCISE 7   Freewriting

Freewrite for five minutes on how you learn best. Think about a time when you learned something successfully.

- What made that experience successful and rewarding?
- Use examples from that experience to describe how you prefer to learn.
- Do you learn best by reading? Listening? Taking notes? Watching a demonstration? Trying to do something new by yourself?

☐ Focusing and Organizing

SPOTLIGHT ON WRITING SKILLS

The Topic Sentence

A very important step in focusing and organizing is deciding on a topic sentence. The topic sentence acts as a road map for the reader, and it covers all of the main (or key) ideas that will be explained in the paragraph.

In deciding on a topic sentence, Kenaane looked at her freewriting (below) and decided which words and ideas seemed to be the most important in describing how she learns. As you can see in her freewriting, she underlined these **keywords**:*

writing words down many times
read it many times
quiet place
group work

Student Freewriting Sample 3

I am not sure what my learning style is and I never heard this word before. But I know the best way for me to learn is by <u>writing words down many times</u>. Then when I hear the word I memorize that word. Sometimes I just <u>read it many times</u>. When I study I like a very quiet place most time in my house when I am alone. I study after class when I get home before I went to work. Sometimes I got up early in the morning before I come to school to study. I never study after work because when I get home it is always late and I am always tired. My job is really difficult because I have to wait on customers and my boss, he always say the customer is all ways right, so I have to apologize when customers are rude or sometimes say sorry. So when I come home to my apartment at night I am too tired to study. <u>Group work</u> is ok if the group is a good group and they are serious. I don't like groups that just talk. But last week when we were working in a group we helped each other by reading the words and then the other person writes them down and then we check them and that was help to me. I did good on the test because we practice as a group.

Kenaane

(Continued)

Finally, she began to see a pattern. She decided that *writing down words many times* and *read it many times* both meant that she repeats things to learn them. She combined the two phrases into one: *repeat things.* Then she added a few words to each of the other phrases to make them clearer (*study in a quiet place* and *work in a serious group*).

Then, Kenaane wrote a topic sentence to include all of these important ideas.

Topic Sentence: The best ways for me to learn are by repeating, studying in a quiet place, and working in a serious group.

EXERCISE 8 Evaluating topic sentences

Here are some topic sentences that students have used to write about the topic of learning styles. Work with a partner. Decide if each topic sentence would be a good road map for a paragraph (Yes or No) and give your reason. Compare your answers with those of another pair of students. The first one has been completed for you.

Yes   (No)   **1.** My learning styles.

            This looks like a title, not a topic sentence.

            In fact, it isn't a sentence.

Yes   No   **2.** I began college in 2002.

            _____

Yes   No   **3.** I once had a teacher who really understood my learning style.

            _____

Yes   No   **4.** Study hard for tests and do your homework.

            _____

Yes   No   **5.** Don't cheat!

            _____

Yes   No   **6.** Since I began college, I have had to change my style of learning.

            _____

EXERCISE 9   **Developing your topic sentence**

Look at your freewriting again. Circle the keywords or ideas. List them here:

1. _____

2. _____

3. _____

Now try to combine them into a topic sentence that will be a road map for the paragraph explaining your learning preference:

Topic Sentence: _____

_____

_____

EXERCISE 10   **Reviewing topic sentences**

Exchange topic sentences with a classmate and check for each other:

- ■ *Circle the keywords in the sentence.*

- ■ *Underline the subject and the verb in the sentence.*

If your classmate could not find keywords or a subject and verb, keep working on your topic sentence until it has keywords and a subject and verb.

SPOTLIGHT ON WRITING SKILLS

Choosing Ideas and Details

Writing is about choosing among many ideas and details to get the ones that best support your main idea. A paragraph is not freewriting! To write a good paragraph, you must not include ideas or details that are not important to your topic sentence. Read Kenaane's freewriting and notice the ideas and details she removed.

Here is some information that
Kenaane decided to leave out,
as she planned her paragraph.

Student Sample 3

I am not sure what my learning style is and I never
heard this word before. But I know the best way for me to
learn is by writing words down many times. Then when I
hear the word I memorize that word. Sometimes I just
read it many times. When I study I like very quiet place
most time in my house when I am alone. I study after class
when I get home before I went to work. Sometimes I got
up early in the morning before I came to school to study.
**I never study after work because when I get home it
is always late and I am always tired. My job is really
difficult because I have to wait on the customers and
my boss, he always say the customer is all ways right,
so I have to apologize when customers are rude or
sometimes say sorry.** So when I come home to my
apartment at night I am too tired to study. Group work is
ok if the group is a good group and they are serious. I
don't like groups that just talk. But last week when we
working in a group we helped each other by reading the
words and then the other person writes them down and
then we check them and that was help to me. I did good
on the test because we practice as a group.

Kenaane

I will leave out this idea or detail	because ...
I never study after work because when I get home it is always late and I am always tired.	This explains why I don't study late in the day, but I already said that I study early in the morning, so this sentence is not needed.
My job is really difficult, I have to wait on the customers and my boss ... sorry.	It doesn't tell readers anything about my learning style.

EXERCISE **11** **Focusing your ideas and details**

Reread your freewriting and ask yourself which details or ideas are not important. Are there any details you should have included but did not? Complete this chart to show any details you decide to leave out or to add.

I will leave out this idea or detail	because ...

I will add this idea or detail	because ...

EXERCISE 12   **Organizing Kenaane's paragraph**

*Each keyword or idea in your topic sentence must be explained in the paragraph. The sentences that explain the keywords are called **supporting sentences**.* Kenaane organized the supporting ideas in a Paragraph Organization Table to make sure she explained each keyword in her topic sentence. Use Kenaane's freewriting (on p. 50) to complete the columns below. The first point she makes, about repetition, has been completed for you.*

Paragraph organization table		
Topic sentence: The best ways for me to learn are by <u>repetition</u>, <u>studying in a quiet place</u>, and <u>working in a serious group</u>.		
Keyword Repetition	**Keywords** Study in a quiet place	**Keywords** Work in a serious group
(support)	**(support)**	**(support)**
▪ Write words down many times		
▪ Read things many times		
▪ Listen and memorize		

EXERCISE **13** **Organizing your paragraph**

Fill in the chart below to organize the information in your freewriting to explain and answer questions about each keyword.

- You may have two, three, or four keywords.
- The number of details to support or explain each keyword may be different.

Paragraph organization table		
Topic sentence:		
Keyword(s)	**Keyword(s)**	**Keyword(s)**
Support for keywords	**Support for keywords**	**Support for keywords**
▪	▪	▪
▪	▪	▪
▪	▪	▪

SPOTLIGHT ON WRITING SKILLS

The Concluding Sentence

A concluding sentence leaves the reader with an important thought. It may do one or more of the following:

- *summarize* what the writer has already said
- make a *recommendation* for the reader
- make a *prediction*
- offer a *solution* to a problem

EXERCISE 14   Reviewing Kenaane's concluding sentences

Kenaane considered each of these concluding sentences. Can you tell which kind each is? The first has been completed for you.

1. I think that if I find other ways to learn faster, I will improve my

   English. *prediction* _____

2. These three techniques seem to work best for me.

   _____

3. I recommend my three favorite ways of learning for any college

   student. _____

4. I can't study if it's noisy, I'm tired, or the group isn't serious, so I

   avoid these situations. _____

   If you guess that 2 is a *summary*, 3 is a *recommendation*, and 4 is a *solution*, you are right.

EXERCISE 15   Writing your concluding sentence

Decide on a concluding sentence for your own paragraph. Write it here:

_____

_____

_____

What does your concluding sentence do?

_____ Summarize

_____ Recommend

_____ Predict

_____ Solve a problem

☐ Writing, Editing, and Revising

SPOTLIGHT ON WRITING SKILLS

Using *Academic Format** Standards

College writing requires that you follow format standards that may be different from what you are used to. Most college classes have standards like these:

Academic Format Standards

- ■ Type or neatly handwrite on one side of the paper.
- ■ Use $8\frac{1}{2} \times 11$ paper.
- ■ Write your name, class, date, and anything else your instructor requires in the proper place (usually the upper right-hand corner of the paper).
- ■ If you use loose-leaf paper, holes go on the left side.
- ■ Leave a 1" margin on the left and at least a $\frac{1}{2}$" margin on the right.
- ■ Indent only the first sentence of the paragraph.

EXERCISE 16   **Using Academic Format Standards**

Now you have planned each part of your paragraph. Write your first draft, putting together the topic sentence, the supporting ideas and details, and the conclusion. Follow the Academic Format Standards.

SPOTLIGHT ON WRITING SKILLS

Editing

A very important part of college writing is rereading what you have written to check for mistakes in grammar, punctuation, and spelling. You edited *sentences* in Chapter 1. Now you will edit entire *paragraphs*. Sometimes it is easier to edit your work if you look for one specific problem at a time. For example, first check your writing to see if the verbs agree with the subjects.

EXERCISE 17 **Editing for subject-verb agreement**

Underline each subject and each verb in your paragraph. Does each verb agree with its subject? How did you do? Check one:

——— I checked all verbs and found no problems.

——— I found verbs that didn't agree with their subjects, and I fixed them.

——— I checked all verbs but am not sure if they agree with their subjects.
      (If you checked this answer, ask a classmate or your instructor for help.)

WEB POWER

You will find additional exercises related to the content in this chapter at **http://esl.college.hmco.com/students**.

EXERCISE 18 **Practicing peer review of a paragraph**

It is a good idea to ask a classmate to look at your writing at this point. You have already done peer reviews of classmates' sentences. For a paragraph, however, peer review may seem more difficult. It helps to use a checklist. With a partner, read Kenaane's **first draft**.* *Complete the Paragraph Checklist together.*

Kenaane A.
ESL 011-01
October 29, 200_
My Learning Preferences

> The best <u>ways</u> for me to learn <u>is</u> by repetition, studying in a quiet place, and working in a serious group. Whether I write, read, or say something I am trying to learn, I have to do it many times. Then I remember it. I can't do this in a noisy place. <u>It have</u> to be quiet. Sometimes I got up early in the morning to study before I go to school because it is quiet and I wasn't tired. I can't study when I am tired from working. I can learn by working in a group, too. But <u>the group have</u> to be serious so I don't waste my time. For example, last week we practice writing vocabulary words in my group. Then I did well on the test because the group work helps me. I think if I find other ways to learn faster, I will improve my English.

Paragraph checklist

1. Is there a topic sentence that has the keywords?   ____ Yes   ____ No

2. Are there enough details or examples to ____ Yes   ____ No
   explain the keywords in the topic sentence?

3. Is there a concluding sentence with an ____ Yes   ____ No
   interesting thought?

4. Does the paragraph follow the Academic ____ Yes   ____ No
   Format Standards?

5. Do the underlined verbs agree with ____ Yes   ____ No
   the subjects?

Write one specific thing that you agree or disagree with in the paragraph:

_____

_____

_____

_____

EXERCISE 19   **Correcting subject-verb agreement problems**

Did you and your partner check No for question 5? You are right. Kenaane had problems with subject-verb agreement. Write the correct verb form for each problem. (Choose a form of either be *or* have.*) Underline the subject in each case:*

1. The best ways for me to learn _____ by repetition,

   studying in a quiet place, and working in a serious group.

2. It _____ to be quiet.

3. But the group _____ to be serious, so I don't

   waste my time.

EXERCISE 20   Using the right tense for the right meaning

Look at these sentences in Kenaane's paragraph and decide if she is talking about now or sometime in the past.

	Kenaane's sentence	Now	Sometime in the past
1	Sometimes I <u>got up</u> early in the morning to study before I <u>go</u> to school because it <u>is</u> quiet and I <u>wasn't</u> tired.		
2	For example, last week we <u>practice</u> writing vocabulary words in my group.		
3	Then I <u>did</u> well on the test because the group work <u>helps</u> me.		

You can check your answers by reading the Power Grammar tip and looking at the examples.

POWER GRAMMAR

Using the Right Tense for the Right Meaning: Present or Past?

Decide which time (or tense) you should use, and don't shift from one time to another without a reason. Some words are clues for the time period and help you decide which verb tense to use. They also help the reader understand when something took place.

Some words that usually mean present time or tense: *today, always, this week, all the time, right now, at this moment, now, sometimes, usually, often.* Usually we use present tense for habits.

Sometimes I get up early in the morning before I go to school because it is quiet and I am not tired.

Some words that usually mean past time or tense: *yesterday, last year, last week, a year ago, the day before yesterday, a few minutes ago.*

Last week we practiced writing vocabulary words in my group.

Then I did well on the test because the group work helped me.

EXERCISE 21 **Editing for the right tense**

Now check your own paragraph and see if you used the correct tense for your meaning. What did you find?

_____ All the tenses are correct.

_____ I found errors and corrected them.

_____ I am not certain if the tenses are correct. I need help from my classmates or instructor.

Write here any sentences you need help on:

_____

_____

_____

_____

_____

_____

_____

_____

EXERCISE 22 **Reviewing with a peer**

Now exchange paragraphs with another student. In the appendix, find Paragraph Checklist 2-1, tear it out, and use it to review each other's writing. Discuss your comments with your classmate. Listen to your classmate's comments on your paragraph.

EXERCISE 23 Thinking about your reaction to peer review

Before you revise your paragraph, think about what your peer reviewer said about it. Circle all words that describe your reaction:

Surprised   Discouraged   Pleased   Disappointed

Unhappy   Angry   Shocked   Resentful

All of these are adjectives that describe typical student reactions to peer review. Accepting criticism is not easy, but it may be an opportunity for you to improve your paragraph.

Now think about how you felt when you were commenting on your classmate's paragraph:

Did you learn something by commenting on your classmate's paragraph?	Yes	No
Did you find it difficult to offer criticism?	Yes	No
Were you afraid to say what you thought?	Yes	No
Were you afraid of offending the writer?	Yes	No
Were you unsure of what to say?	Yes	No

These, too, are natural reactions for most student writers, but students usually feel better after they have practiced the peer review process. Both partners benefit from peer review!

SPOTLIGHT ON WRITING SKILLS

Revision

To *revise** means to improve your writing's content (what you said) and organization (how you arranged your topic sentence, supporting details, and concluding sentence). You do this after a review by your peers and after your own reflection.

EXERCISE 24 **Revising your paragraph**

Look at your classmate's comments and answers on Paragraph Checklist 2-1. Make changes so that your paragraph is your best work. Then give it to your instructor. You will make more changes later, after your instructor has reviewed the paragraph. You may write a second and even a third draft.

EXERCISE 25 **Thinking about the writing process**

The three-step writing process may be a new experience for you. Answer these questions:

1. Writing the paragraph was:

   _____ easy

   _____ somewhat easy

   _____ hard

2. I spent _____ minutes / hours writing my

   paragraph.

3. In the peer review, two helpful things that my partner said included:

   _____

   _____

   _____

   _____

   _____

   _____

4. The peer review helped me / did not help me improve my

   paragraph.

Writing Assignment 2

This writing assignment has several steps and requires some preparation *before* you actually write. You will explore study strategies to suit your learning styles. You will choose your topic *after* you have completed the preparation steps.

Expanding Your Academic Vocabulary

Some of the language in the Perceptual Learning Preferences Survey and materials may be difficult. But this is an opportunity to expand or improve your academic vocabulary while learning some techniques that will be helpful to you. You have already added two of these words (*visual* and *tactile*) to your Word Bank. Add the others as you learn them.

Gathering Information

EXERCISE 26 **Learning necessary vocabulary**

Your instructor will divide the class into groups for this exercise by assigning you a letter, A, B, C, or D. Which are you? Circle your letter: A B C D. Then follow the directions on page 66. Some steps may be done in class, others at home. Your instructor will give you this information.

visual	verbal	nonverbal	auditory	models
tactile	kinesthetic	strategy	oral	concept

If you are an A:

- Work by yourself.
- Look up each word and write down its meaning.
- Learn the words by yourself by studying them quietly and by writing them many times—but not by saying them out loud.

If you are a B:

- Work by yourself.
- Look up each word and write it and its meaning on a flash card.
- Use the flash cards to quiz yourself on the words.

If you are a C:

- Work with one or two other Cs.
- Look up each word and write it and its meaning on a flash card.
- Use the flash cards to quiz each other on the words.

If you are a D:

- Work with the other Ds, not by yourself.
- With the group, look up the definitions of the words, but do not write them down.
- Practice by repeating the words and their meanings to each other.
- If a group member has a tape recorder, you may record the words and definitions and listen to the tape to study.

EXERCISE 27 Testing yourself on the vocabulary

| visual | verbal | nonverbal | auditory | models |
| tactile | kinesthetic | strategy | oral | concept |

Your instructor will read the ten words to you. Write each word, and then write its definition. Check them yourself. How did you do? Write the number you got right here: _____ .

Be sure to add the ten terms to your Word Bank.

EXERCISE 28   Discussing vocabulary study methods

How comfortable were you with the way you were required to study the vocabulary? Answer the questions below. Then discuss your answers with your classmates.

- Was it difficult or easy to follow the directions?
- Would you normally learn vocabulary the way you were assigned, if you had a choice?
- Did you learn a new technique that you have never used before?
- Would you have done better on the test if you could have used your own strategies?

EXERCISE 29   Completing the preferences survey

Now take a survey that may give you more insight into how you learn. The Perceptual Learning Preferences Survey (Kinsella, 1993) is in Appendix 2, beginning on page 232.

When you have completed the survey, score it, using the instructions and guide at the end of this chapter. Practice first on the scoring guide for a student named Mari:

Mari's Perceptual Learning Preferences Survey: Scoring Guide

DIRECTIONS: Each of the checks Mari entered on the survey has a point value:
USUALLY = 3 points; SOMETIMES = 2 points; RARELY = 1 point

For each column, find the item number on the survey and enter the point value on the line to the right. Then add the total number of points in each column.

Visual/Verbal		Visual/Nonverbal		Auditory		Visual/Tactile Kinesthetic	
Number	Points	Number	Points	Number	Points	Number	Points
2.	2	4.	3	1.	2	3.	1
6.	3	7.	3	5.	3	8.	1
10.	1	14.	1	9.	1	11.	3
16.	2	17.	3	12.	2	13.	1
21.	3	19.	3	15.	1	20.	3
25.	3	22.	1	18.	2	24.	2
30.	3	26.	1	23.	2	28.	3
32.	3	29.	3	27.	2	31.	2
	Total: 20		Total: 18		Total: 15		Total: 16

In the space below, list Mari's perceptual learning preferences, from her highest score to her lowest score. Her highest total indicates her perceptual learning preference(s). Mari's next highest total indicates another strong preference, especially if the two numbers are close.

Perceptual learning preferences for Mari:

1. _Visual/Verbal (20 points)_

2. _Visual/Nonverbal (18 points)_

3. _Visual/Tactile Kinesthetic (16 points)_

4. _Auditory (15 points)_

EXERCISE 30 **Checking your comprehension**

Answer these questions about Mari's learning style preferences.

1. What is Mari's <u>strongest</u> learning preference? _____

2. What is her <u>weakest</u> learning preference? _____

EXERCISE 31 **Understanding your learning style**

You have taken the Perceptual Learning Preferences Survey. You have scored it. Now locate the sections of information for your learning style preferences on the Web at http://esl.college.hmco.com/students. Look at characteristics for your learning style preferences. Then look at "Teaching Strategies to Help You Learn" and "Study Strategies to Help You Remember." Read them and make notes for any that interest you. (You may want to look up some words and add them to your Word Bank.)

EXERCISE 32 **Discussing your learning style survey results**

Write the answers to these questions. Then discuss your answers with a classmate.

- Do the results of this survey agree with your ideas about how you learn best?

  _____

  _____

- Do the *characteristics* accurately describe you? Were you surprised at the results?

  _____

- What did you learn about yourself that you didn't know?

  _____

  _____

- Which suggested *Study Strategies to Help You Remember* have you tried?

  _____

  _____

- Which do you want to try?

  _____

  _____

EXERCISE 33 **Making a study strategy plan**

Develop a study strategy plan for yourself, based on your understanding of your learning style preferences. (The Study Strategy Plan form 2-2 is in the appendix.)

For example, a student named Marcella is an auditory learner. She learns best by listening. She discovered she is already using some strategies that help auditory learners, and she found several other strategies she would like to try. Here is her plan:

Study strategy plan
Name: *Marcella*
My major learning strength(s): *Auditory*
Study strategies I already use: ■ *I make flashcards for new vocabulary.* ■ *I summarize what I want to learn aloud to myself or to a friend.*
Study strategies I would like to try: ■ *I will ask Maria to be my "study buddy" to prepare for tests.* ■ *I will tape-record my class notes and listen to them in the car on my way to work.*

▭ Focusing and Organizing

EXERCISE 34 Focusing on one topic

You have gathered much information about your learning styles. Now use some of the information from your survey and your Study Strategy Plan to write a paragraph on one *of these topics. Check the topic you choose:*

Topics

_____ Describe some examples of two or three new strategies you plan to try to become a better student.

_____ Describe the teaching style of the best instructor you have ever had. Explain how the instructor's teaching strategies worked well for you.

_____ When you studied the vocabulary in Exercise 25, did the method you used seem natural to you? Was it the strategy recommended based on The Perceptual Learning Preferences Survey? Explain.

EXERCISE 35 Freewriting on your topic

Freewrite for five minutes about your topic. Include any ideas that come to mind. Do not worry about spelling, grammar, or punctuation.

EXERCISE 36 Using keywords to plan your topic sentence

Read your freewriting.

Cross out any ideas or details not related to your topic. Add more ideas or details if you think of any.

Then circle any words in your freewriting that seem most important or key to what you want to say. Write them here:

1. _____

2. _____

3. _____

Write your topic sentence here:

_____

_____

EXERCISE 37 **Reviewing topic sentences**

Exchange topic sentences with a partner.

- Circle the key ideas in your partner's topic sentence.
- Underline the subject and the verb.
- Does the verb agree with the subject?

Return the topic sentence to your partner and give any advice you have on how to improve it.

EXERCISE 38 **Organizing your paragraph**

Use the Paragraph Organization Table to organize your supporting details for each keyword.

Paragraph organization table		
Topic sentence:		
Keyword(s)	**Keyword(s)**	**Keyword(s)**
Support for this keyword:	**Support for this keyword:**	**Support for this keyword:**
▪	▪	▪
▪	▪	▪
▪	▪	▪

EXERCISE 39 Writing your concluding sentence

Write your concluding sentence here:

_____

_____

What does your concluding sentence do?

_____ Summarize

_____ Recommend

_____ Predict

_____ Solve a problem

⬜ Writing, Editing, and Revising

EXERCISE 40 Using Academic Format Standards

Now write your paragraph. Remember to follow the Academic Format Standards. Review them by filling in the blanks.

- Type or neatly handwrite on _____ side of the paper.

- Use 8½" × 11" _____.

- Write your _____, class, _____, and anything else your instructor requires in the proper place (usually the upper right-hand corner of the paper).

- If you use loose-leaf paper, _____ go on the _____ side.

- Leave a 1" _____ on the left and at least a ½" margin on the _____.

- Indent only the _____ sentence of the paragraph.

EXERCISE **41**   **Editing your paragraph**

Before you give your paragraph to your instructor, look at it carefully.

Underline or highlight all the subjects and verbs.

Now ask yourself these Power Grammar questions and circle your answers:

- Does each clause have a subject and a verb?   Yes   No

- Does each verb agree with its subject?   Yes   No

- Did you choose the correct verb tense for the meaning? Yes   No

If you are not sure about some of your answers, what could you do?
List two possibilities. Then do one or both of them.

1. I could _____.

2. I could _____.

EXERCISE **42**   **Doing a peer review**

Do you remember that you had a choice of four topics? Find someone in your class who wrote on the same topic as you. Exchange paragraphs with that person. Using the Peer Review Form 2-3 in the appendix, review your partner's writing.

Make any changes to your paragraph before you hand it in to your instructor; base your changes on the peer review and your partner's comments. Your instructor will make further suggestions to improve your paragraph.

▭ Additional Topics for More Practice and Assessment

Topics for Timed or Independent Writing

- Compare the difficulty of writing in English with the difficulty of writing in your first language. Explain what makes writing in English more (or less) difficult for you.
- Many people believe that today's students do not write as well as students did a generation ago. They blame poor writing skills on too much television, video games, and not enough reading. What do you think? Explain your answer fully.

- Has your learning style changed since you were a child? Explain and give examples.
- Does everyone in your family seem to have the same learning style? Explain and give examples.
- Write about your favorite technique for learning vocabulary or mathematics. Describe it in detail.
- How is the writing process you are learning in this chapter different from or similar to a writing process you have used in the past? Which do you prefer?
- Writing, reading, and speaking English are all challenges. Which is the most challenging for you and why?
- In your first language, did you enjoy writing more or less than writing in English? Why?
- Natural talents make it easy for some people to learn a skill. For example, some athletes, like David Beckham, seem to be "naturals" at soccer or other sports. Describe one natural talent you have and describe how it has made learning in that area easy for you.
- Identical twins often have similar talents, interests, and learning styles. If you know any twins, discuss whether you agree or disagree with this statement. Give examples to show the reader how the twins are similar or different.
- Do you think hard work or intelligence is more important to success in college? Write a paragraph to explain your answer and support it with examples.

Projects

- Find another learning styles inventory or questionnaire. Look on the Internet (try http://esl.college.hmco.com/students) for a start, and type in *learning styles* as the keywords). Compare your results on the inventory with your results on the Perceptual Learning Preferences Survey. Are they similar or different? Write a paragraph explaining your answer.
- Make another copy of the Perceptual Learning Preferences Survey. Have a friend take it, and help her or him score the survey and interpret the results. You are the expert! Write a paragraph describing your friend's results.

▭ Reflection on Chapter 2

EXERCISE 43 **Evaluating yourself**

Now that you have completed Chapter 2, **reflect on your learning** *for each objective. Check the box with the statement that applies to you.*

Objective	This was <u>new</u> to me.	I learned <u>more</u> about this than I knew before.	I need to learn more about this.
Identify your learning style preferences			
Understand subject-verb agreement			
Use the correct verb tense for the right meaning (present or past?)			
Use a three-step writing process for a paragraph:			
1. Gather information			
2. Focus and organize			
3. Write, edit, and revise			

If you are still having problems with a Chapter 2 objective, try some of these suggestions:

- Review the Power Grammar.
- You will find additional exercises related to the content in this chapter at http://esl.college.hmco.com/students.
- Talk to your instructor about getting more help.
- See if your college has a writing center, a learning laboratory, or tutoring services for students. If you can find a place where you can receive help, make an appointment to visit.
- Try studying with a classmate who has mastered some point you are finding troublesome.

WEB POWER

You will find additional exercises related to the content in this chapter at http://esl.college.hmco.com/students.

Who Will You Be?
Setting Goals and
Making Decisions

Academic Writing Objectives

- Distinguish between general and specific details
- Use infinitives, check for parallel structure
- Control the tone of your writing
- Write more powerful sentences
- Organize your paragraph—choices

Here is what to expect in this chapter:

You will write a paragraph on	For the purpose of	Focus on these writing skills	Learning this Power Grammar	Using these graphic organizers	With this vocabulary focus
A specific goal and how you will reach it	Description	General vs. specific	Infinitives in academic writing	Goal planning form	Try unfamiliar words
		Add a "hook"		Outline	Linking words
The real you	Description	Use details	Parallel structure	Outline	Details make writing come to life
		Write strong sentences		Peer review forms	
Decision making using matrices	Analysis	Control tone	Vocabulary for controlling tone	Decision matrices	Necessary vocabulary: criterion/ criteria, matrix/ matrices
	Cause and effect			Ways to organize paragraphs	

Writing Assignment 1

For this assignment, you will write a paragraph about a goal and describe the steps you will use to achieve it. You will follow the steps of Gathering Information, Focusing and Organizing, and Writing, Editing, and Revising that you practiced in Chapter 2.

▭ Gathering Information

EXERCISE 1 Dreaming of the future

In Chapter 1, you described yourself as a high school student. Now, with a partner, dream about your future.

Take turns answering these questions. Use your imagination!

- Describe what you will be like in one year. How will you be different from who you are today?

- Imagine your life in five years. What will you be doing? Where will you be?

- Describe the person you want to be ten years from now. What will your life be like?

What kinds of goals did you describe to your partner? Check all that apply:

_____ career goals

_____ academic goals

_____ personal relationship goals

_____ financial goals

EXERCISE **2** **Reading about student goals**

*Here are some of the goals students have written about. Read each
paragraph and decide what kinds of goals each student has. Each student
may have more than one goal. Put an X next to your answers and underline
where each goal appears. The first paragraph has been completed for you.*

Student Sample 1 (Victor)

I have two important reasons to stay in the United States
of America, <u>learn english</u> and <u>study construction surveying</u>. First,
learning English is essential if I wish to <u>get a better life</u> and to be
a surveyor. Learning English will make me feel comfortable and
able to write, read, and communicate with other people. If I learn
English very well I will be able to take surveying classes at this
college. Second, in the future I want to <u>be a surveyor and work in
a construction company</u>. I know that it is hard to get my goal in
this country, but it is not impossible to do; therefore, I have to
study very hard.

Victor

_X_ Career Goal   _X_ Educational Goal

_X_ Personal Goal   ____ Financial Goal

Student Sample 2 (Ijaz)

I have some goals for my future and for my family. First, I
have an educational goal. I want to start regular college study at
this college, and I want to study Information Systems Technology.
Then I want a better job. Then I have some goals for my family. I
want to support them. We are living in an apartment. I want to
buy a house, I want to feed my family, and I want to provide
better education for my brother and sisters. I am very happy that
I have the same goals that my father has. In five years I will be
able to fulfill my desire for a better job, and I will be married.

Ijaz

____ Career Goal   ____ Educational Goal

____ Personal Goal   ____ Financial Goal

Student Sample 3 (Karim)

My goal is to succeed in my life. I don't have any special career in my dream because I'm going to do my best to be happy in the future. I'll try to have a good job, and I wish to meet a good and nice girl to marry and spend the rest of my life with her.

Karim

____ Career Goal   ____ Educational Goal

____ Personal Goal   ____ Financial Goal

Student Sample 4 (Ana)

In life I have many goals. Some of them are short term. Others are in a long period of time. Still other goals are a dream because it is difficult to achieve them. For me, a goal is a path. My goals in the short term are: I want to know how to drive a car so I can be an independent person. I want to learn how to speak English clearly, think in English, and write correctly. I want to make interesting conversation when people speak English with me, by phone or in meetings. I want to work and find an interesting job for practicing my English. My goals for the long term: I want to buy a house with a big yard for my children to play and run around in. Another goal is to see my children work as professionals. I think my most important and most ambitious goal is someday I want to work in a hospital with sick children so that I can help them. I think goals are like dreams, and dreams sometimes come true, but sometimes they are only dreams. Nevertheless, I have to try in spite of adversities.

Ana

____ Career Goal   ____ Educational Goal

____ Personal Goal   ____ Financial Goal

EXERCISE 3   Making goals specific

Now decide whether each student's goals are specific (detailed) or general (lacking in details).

- Is the goal clear because of details (facts, examples, experience, description)?
- Or is the goal vague and unclear because of lack of details?

Put an X in the box for each goal.

	Career goal		Educational goal		Personal goal		Financial goal	
	Specific	General	Specific	General	Specific	General	Specific	General
Victor	X		X			X		
Ijaz								
Karim								
Ana								

EXERCISE 4   Discussing your answers

With one or two classmates, discuss your answers to these questions. Of course, the answers to many of these questions may be different from student to student. There is no right or wrong answer. But you should be able to give reasons for your answers.

1. _____ Which student has the greatest number of general goals?

2. _____ Which student has the greatest number of specific goals?

3. _____ Which student has no specific goals? Is this paragraph less interesting because it does not have supporting details?

4. _____ Which is the clearest paragraph?

5. _____ What makes it clearest? Is it the details and specific information?

EXERCISE 5   **Comparing your answers**

Using the blackboard to record the votes, take a vote in your class on which paragraph is overall best, clearest, and most interesting to read. Which paragraph had the most votes?

——   Victor's paragraph

——   Ijaz's paragraph

——   Karim's paragraph

——   Ana's paragraph

For the winning paragraph, write a few notes about why your classmates chose it:

_____'s paragraph got the most votes because

_____

_____

_____

_____

_____

_____

_____

_____

Many readers say that lots of details bring writing to life so that they can understand and enjoy it.

EXERCISE 6   **Freewriting about your goal**

You described your goals to a partner in Exercise 1. Now freewrite for five minutes about one of your goals for the future. It could be a career, educational, personal, or financial goal. Remember: write without stopping to correct your grammar, spelling, or punctuation.

▭ **Focusing and Organizing**

Organizing the steps for achieving your goal will help you focus and add details. Ana completed the Goal Planning Step by Step form for one of her specific goals.

Ana's goal planning step by step		
My specific goal: My specific goal is to get a driver's license so that I can be independent.		
Step 1	Save enough money and buy a car	Complete by: End of November 2005
Step 2	Get my learner's permit	Complete by: End of December 2005
Step 3	Take a class to learn how to drive	Complete by: End of January 2006
Step 4	Take the road test to get my driver's license	Complete by: End of February 2006

EXERCISE 7 **Evaluating Ana's goal plan**

With a partner, answer these questions about Ana's plan. If you answer No to any question, be ready to explain why.

1. Does Ana's plan have enough steps?   Yes   No, because _____

_____

_____ .

2. Are the steps in a logical order?   Yes   No, because _____

_____

_____ .

3. Did Ana allow enough time to complete each step?   Yes   No, because

_____

_____ .

EXERCISE 8 **Making your own goal plan**

Use the Goal Planning Step by Step form to focus your details. If you have more than six steps, add spaces at the bottom of the form. There is also a copy in the appendix that you may use. (Remember: detail is good!)

Goal Planning Step By Step		
My specific goal:		
Step 1		Complete by: (date)
Step 2		Complete by:
Step 3		Complete by:
Step 4		Complete by:
Step 5		Complete by:
Step 6		Complete by:

EXERCISE 9 **Evaluating goal plans**

Show your Goal Planning Step by Step form to another student. Ask your partner to answer these questions and give reasons for any No answers:

- Does the plan have enough steps?

  Yes   No, because _____.

- Are the steps in a logical order?

  Yes   No, because _____.

- Is enough time allowed for each step?

  Yes   No, because _____.

Discuss your answers with your partner. Change your plan to improve it.

EXERCISE **10** **Writing your topic sentence**

The topic sentence can be your <u>goal assessment</u> in the Goal Planning Step by Step box. For example, Ana's topic sentence is, My <u>specific goal is to get a driver's license so that I can be independent</u>.

Write your topic sentence here:

_____

_____

SPOTLIGHT ON WRITING SKILLS

Using a "Hook"

Although the topic sentence is usually the first sentence in a paragraph, some writers begin with a sentence that is designed to interest the reader. This is called a *hook*.* (Think of a fishhook with bait to catch the fish!)

For example, Ana started her paragraph with this sentence: "When I arrived in the USA, I noticed cars are like feet because they get you everywhere you need to go." Then she wrote her topic sentence: "My specific goal is to get a driver's license so that I can be independent."

EXERCISE **11** **Adding a "hook"**

Can you think of a "hook" for your paragraph that will interest your readers? Write some possibilities here:

_____

_____

_____

_____

_____

_____

EXERCISE 12   **Organizing major points and details**

Use the steps you wrote in the Goal Planning Step by Step form for the major points in your paragraph. Each step must be a complete sentence. (You may have only four or five points.)

List your supporting details as 1 and 2 under each major point. The details will help the reader understand each step you plan to follow to achieve your specific goal. Details also make the writing more interesting.

Topic Sentence _____

_____

    A. Major Point/Step

        _____

        _____

        1. Supporting Detail:

          _____

        2. Supporting Detail:

          _____

    B. Major Point/Step

        _____

        _____

        1. Supporting Detail:

          _____

        2. Supporting Detail:

          _____

    C. Major Point/Step

        _____

        _____

        1. Supporting Detail:

          _____

    2. Supporting Detail:

    _____

D. Major Point/Step

  _____

  _____

    1. Supporting Detail:

    _____

    2. Supporting Detail:

    _____

E. Major Point/Step

  _____

  _____

    1. Supporting Detail:

    _____

    2. Supporting Detail:

    _____

F. Major Point/Step

  _____

  _____

    1. Supporting Detail:

    _____

    2. Supporting Detail:

    _____

> ### Linking Words*
>
> Good writers help their readers understand the relationships between their ideas by using words to link them. For this writing assignment, you will need words that tell the *order* in which you will do the steps.

EXERCISE 13 **Trying some linking verbs**

Think about how you will link the ideas in your paragraph. You need words that tell the order in which you will do the steps. Choose two or three in each group below to write some main points for your paragraph. Use the blanks to try out some sentences for your paragraph.

GROUP 1: You could use **ordinal numbers*** that show the order of things.

First, _____

First of all, _____

The **first** thing I will do _____

The **first** step _____

Second, _____

The **second** step I will take is _____

My **third** step _____

Fourth, I plan to _____

GROUP 2: You could use other words to keep the reader on track:

The **next** thing _____

After that, _____

Then, _____

GROUP 3: To end the paragraph, you might choose:

Finally, _____

In conclusion, _____

Can you think of any other words to show what happens first? Write

them here: _____

EXERCISE 14 **Finding linking words in Victor's paragraph**

With a partner, look for and circle all the linking words that tell the order of the steps in Victor's paragraph.

Student Sample 5 (Victor)

My Specific Goal

My specific goal in the future is to get a certificate as a surveyor. (First,) I have to finish my ESL classes. Then I will be able to take construction surveying classes at Alexandria Community College (ACC). Therefore, I'm studying very hard with English. I sometimes make mistakes, but I don't feel disappointed about that because I'm learning English. In two years, I will be able to read, write, and speak English well. Second, I'm going to take construction surveying classes at ACC. I want to finish construction surveying in one year. I know that I can do it because I have knowledge about construction surveying. In the future, after I graduate as a surveyor, I would like to work in a big construction company, especially in highway construction or bridge construction. I would like to buy a surveyor's instrument and begin to work by myself. I like working by myself. I'd like to return to my country and to teach surveying to others.

Victor

EXERCISE 15 **Finding concluding sentences**

Here is Ana's paragraph. Read it and answer the questions that follow it.

Student Sample 6 (Ana)

My "Feet" in America

When I arrived in the USA, I noticed cars are like feet because they get you everywhere you need to go. But I don't know how to drive. My specific goal is to get a driver's license so that I can be independent. I want to learn how to do it although I don't have a car. My first step is to make money and to buy a car by November 2005. Then in December 2005 I will study for the written test and go to the DMV to get my learner's permit. Then, in January 2006, I will take a class and I will begin to learn how to drive. After practicing, I can take the road test to get my driver's license by the end of February 2006. After that I will become an independent woman, so I can go wherever I want without a wait or bothering someone. In conclusion, in America I have to drive. Driving is a tool, like our feet in this huge country.

Ana

Answer these questions:

■ Find the concluding sentences in Ana's paragraph (she has two).

Write them here: _____

_____

■ Circle the connecting words that signal to the reader that she is

concluding her paragraph. Write the words here: _____

_____

■ What does Ana's conclusion do?

_____ summarize

_____ make a recommendation

_____ predict

_____ offer a solution

EXERCISE 16   **Writing your concluding sentence**

Write a concluding sentence for your paragraph.

_____

What does it do for the reader?

- It summarizes what I said.
- It makes a recommendation.
- It makes a prediction.
- It offers a solution to a problem.

🔲 Writing, Editing, and Revising

EXERCISE 17   **Writing your first draft**

Write your first draft, following the Academic Format Standards.

EXERCISE 18   **Editing your draft**

Now reread your draft and check it for any errors. If you are not sure how to answer, review the Power Grammar point, which may be in Chapters 1 and 2. Write an X when you have completed each editing task.

_____ My sentences are complete. (Chapter 1)

_____ All the verbs agree with the subjects. (Chapter 2)

_____ I chose the correct tense for the meaning. (Chapter 2)

_____ All sentences begin with capital letters and end with periods or other punctuation. (Chapter 1)

> **Master Student Tip**
>
> Good writers often put their first draft aside and leave it for a period of time, from one hour to one day. Then they can look at it with "fresh eyes" and make changes they couldn't do when they had just finished writing.

EXERCISE 19   **Completing a peer review**

Exchange paragraphs with another student. Use Peer Review Form 3-1 in the appendix to review your classmate's draft. When you have made your comments, discuss them with the writer, and listen to the comments on your draft paragraph.

EXERCISE 20   **Revising your paragraph**

Considering what you learned from the peer review process, carefully reread your paragraph and make any changes you think will improve it. When you are satisfied that your second draft represents your best work, give it to your instructor for further review.

EXERCISE **21** **Circling the infinitives**

Notice the words and phrases in **boldface*** *print in Ana's and Victor's paragraphs below. These are called* infinitives.* *They are often used in academic writing.*

- *With a partner, circle the infinitives in the two paragraphs.*
- *Then read on for a Power Grammar tip about infinitives.*

My "Feet" in America

When I arrived in the USA, I noticed cars are like feet because they get you everywhere you need **to go**. But I don't know how **to drive**. My specific goal is **to get** a driver's license so that I can be independent. I want **to learn** how **to do** it although I don't have a car. My first step is **to make** money and **to buy** a car by November 2004. Then in December 2004 I will study for the written test and go to the DMV to get my learner's permit. Then, in January 2005, I will take a class and I will begin **to learn** how **to drive**. After practicing, I can take the road test to get my driver's license by the end of February 2005. After that I will become an independent woman, so I can go wherever I want without a wait or bothering someone. In conclusion, in America I have **to drive**. Driving is a tool, like our feet in this huge country.

Ana

My Specific Goal

My specific goal in the future is **to get** a certificate as a surveyor. First, I have **to finish** my ESL classes. Then I will be able **to take** construction surveying classes at Alexandria Community College (ACC). Therefore, I'm studying very hard with English. I sometimes make mistakes, but I don't feel disappointed about that because I'm learning English. In two years, I will be able **to read**, **write**, and **speak** English well. Second, I'm going **to take** construction surveying classes at ACC. I want **to finish** construction surveying in one year. I know that I can do it because I have knowledge about construction surveying. In the future, after I graduate as a surveyor, I would like **to work** in a big construction company, especially in highway construction or bridge construction. I would like **to buy** a surveyor's instrument and begin **to work** by myself. I like working by myself. I'd like **to return** to my country and **to teach** surveying to others.

Victor

POWER GRAMMAR

Using Infinitives in Academic Writing

Academic writing uses more infinitives than we use in conversation. (An infinitive is *to* plus **the simple form of a verb**.) Also, seven verbs are used more than any other verbs just before infinitives. So, when you learn to use these seven verbs, you have learned most ways to introduce an infinitive in English.

Academic writing uses this pattern more than we do in talking.	Most students *want* **to finish** college quickly and **to find** jobs with good pay and good benefits.
Seven words are the most commonly used verbs to introduce infinitives: *want, try, seem, like, begin, tend, attempt.*	Many people *seem* **to think** they should know what they *want* **to be** before they finish high school.
Want is used more than any of the others. *Attempt* is used the least, but it is still an important word to learn to use.	But today many people *tend* **to have** more than one career over their lifetimes. In college, students *attempt* **to explore** their interests and possible careers.
Try and *attempt* are used when we write about efforts to do something.	*Try* **to determine** your talents before you consider which area to major in.
Want and *like* are used when we write about our desires.	I *want* **to be** a scientist because I *like* **to figure** out the secrets of the physical world.
Seem and *tend* are used when we write about possibilities and things we think are likely to happen or not likely to happen.	Jerry *seems* **to relax** when he is in the chemistry lab, but I *tend* **to become** anxious.

EXERCISE 22 **Practicing using infinitives**

Look at the words Ana and Victor used with infinitives.

Ana said: I want **to learn** how to do it although I don't have a car.
I will begin **to learn** how to drive.

Victor said: I want **to finish** construction surveying in one year.
I would like **to work** in a big construction company.
I would like **to buy** a surveyor's instrument and **to begin** to work by myself.
I'd like **to return** to my country and **to teach** surveying to others.

As you can see, Ana and Victor used only begin + **infinitive**, want + **infinitive**, and like + **infinitive**. Perhaps they are most comfortable with these three verbs.

What about you? Write sentences using all seven verbs *plus an infinitive:*

1. want:

_____

_____

_____

2. try:

_____

_____

_____

3. seem:

_____

_____

_____

4. like:

_____

_____

_____

5. begin:

_____

_____

_____

6. tend:

_____

_____

_____

7. attempt:

_____

_____

_____

Read your sentences to a partner, and listen to your partner's sentences.
Which of the seven words were most difficult for you and your partner to
use in your sentences? Check them here:

_____ want   _____ try   _____ seem   _____ like

_____ begin   _____ tend   _____ attempt

Using Unfamiliar Words
Make a habit of trying out unfamiliar (or difficult) words when you
learn them. This is a good way to expand your academic vocabulary
with words you understand but may not use when you speak. If you
use them several times, they will be yours.

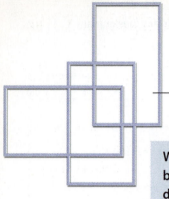

Writing Assignment 2

Whether you are choosing a college major or a career, your decision will be better if you take into consideration the *real* you. If you base your decisions on your natural interests and talents, you will probably do better and get more satisfaction from your study and your career. For this assignment, you will write a paragraph to describe the *real* you.

☐ Gathering Information

EXERCISE 23 Describing yourself

Complete each statement describing yourself.

What I know about myself:

■ I have always enjoyed (*list as many activities as possible*):

_____

_____

_____

■ I am very interested in: _____

■ I love to read about: _____

■ I am happiest when I: _____

■ When I daydream, I imagine myself as: _____

What others say about me:

■ My friends say I am talented at: _____

■ My parents and relatives say I am good at: _____

■ My boss or coworkers say I do well at: _____

■ People who know me have suggested that I would be successful at:

_____

When you completed some statements, you may have made a list of words. Read this Power Grammar tip about writing lists.

POWER GRAMMAR

Parallel Structure in Academic Sentences

To be an academic writer, it is important to learn the style expected by instructors in your academic papers. One feature of that style is that things given in a list all have the same structure. This is a way of saying that the items of the list have to be *parallel* in grammar.

Academic writing uses parallel structure to give lists of items in a sentence. Parallel is like the tracks for a train: both parts run side by side and have the same structure.

Most students want **to finish** college quickly and **to find** jobs with good pay and good benefits.

The first example shows two parallel parts.

Here are examples to show other kinds of parallel grammar.

I have enjoyed **driving** cars, **riding** motorcycles, and **racing** dirt bikes.

I have always loved **cars**, **motorcycles**, and **dirt bikes**.

I am happiest when I am **waiting** on customers, **solving** their problems, and **selling** them the best car for their needs.

Each night, I **eat** dinner, **watch** television, and **do** my homework.

EXERCISE 24   **Correcting for parallel structure**

Find any items that are not parallel in each sentence and correct each.
There may be more than one way to do this. Each item is numbered to help
you. Some sentences have more than one error. There is more than one way
to correct each sentence.

1. I am happiest when I am waiting on customers, answer questions, and
   giving change.

2. My boss says I do well at stocking shelves and take inventory.

3. I feel I need to learn English, a college degree, and getting a job.

4. When I daydream, I think about having enough money so that I
   can go to school full-time, graduating from college, to be a dentist.

5. My parents say I'm good at fixing appliances, working on computers,
   and tune up engines.

6. I have always enjoyed sports, outdoor activities, and to camp in the
   wilderness.

Compare your answers with those of a classmate. How did you do?

_____ I got most of them right.

_____ I need more help with parallel structures.

Focusing and Organizing

EXERCISE 25 **Choosing the most interesting sentences**

Work with a partner. Ask your partner to look at all your sentences from Exercise 23 and to put a check mark next to the two or three most interesting ones. Do the same for your partner. Usually the most interesting sentences are the ones with the most details.

SPOTLIGHT ON WRITING SKILLS

Details Make Writing Come to Life

When you write, you want to communicate with the reader. Details help make that possible by giving the reader enough information so that your ideas come alive. This makes your sentences effective.

For example, which sentence below is more effective? Why?
1. I rode my bike to work in the rain.
2. I rode my new red bike to my job at the coffee shop in the pouring rain.

EXERCISE 26 **Adding details**

Your partner should ask questions about your most interesting sentences to get more details or to make your ideas clearer. For example, look at the sentence in the box:

I am happiest when I am playing sports.

WEAK!

*This sentence is weak. It doesn't give a clear picture of the student. By adding details, the sentence could be strengthened. Ask **the five W and one H questions*** to get more details. For example:*

I am happiest when I am playing sports.	
Who/whom?	with my three best high school friends
What?	doubles tennis
When?	on a rainy day, in the middle of August
Where?	clay court, New Orleans
Why?	to prepare for the citywide tournament
How?	energetically

Of course, you wouldn't put all the details in your sentence, but you could:

STRONG!
(Maybe TOO strong!)

I am happiest when I am playing ~~sports~~ doubles tennis energetically with my three best high school friends on a clay court on a rainy day in the middle of August in New Orleans because we want to prepare for the city-wide tournament.

Now try this process with one of your interesting sentences:

Your sentence:	
Who/whom?	
What?	
When?	
Where?	
Why?	
How?	
Your IMPROVED sentence:	

Now help your partner expand one of her or his sentences by adding details.

EXERCISE 27   **Practicing adding details to sentences**

Expand three of your sentences with additional details by answering the five W and one H questions. Write your expanded, more effective sentences here:

1. _____

2. _____

3. _____

EXERCISE 28   **Writing your topic sentence**

*Think about a topic sentence that will focus your paragraph about yourself. The topic sentence should make a statement about you as a **unique*** person and use some of the keywords and ideas in the sentences you wrote. What qualities or characteristics make you a unique person? Your topic sentence should answer this question.*

EXERCISE 29   **Identifying key ideas for Marcella's topic sentence**

Marcella had these three sentences that contain key or important ideas about her. Read them carefully to understand her ideas.

1. I love working in a restaurant because I can easily deal with people and their problems.
2. I have worked in several businesses while I have been a student.
3. I don't like to read, but I really know how to interact with people.

She looked for a common thread in these sentences, something that combines her qualities or characteristics, to describe herself in a topic sentence. Here are four topic sentences she thought about using. Circle the one you think is the best.

1. I really enjoy working in a restaurant.
2. I am a person who can be very intelligent in a business, especially in a restaurant.
3. I don't like to read books at all.
4. The real me.

Did you choose sentence 2? That is the best answer. Why are the other sentences not good topic sentences?

▪ Which is not really a sentence?   _____

▪ Which are too narrow and don't include key ideas? _____

EXERCISE 30 **Developing your topic sentence**

Write your topic sentence here:

_____

_____

_____

_____

_____

EXERCISE 31 **Doing a peer review of topic sentences**

Exchange your topic sentence with another student. Answer these questions about each other's topic sentence:

1. Does the topic sentence tell you the   Yes   No
   qualities or characteristics that make
   the writer unique?

2. Is the topic sentence a complete sentence?   Yes   No

3. What questions do you expect to be answered in the paragraph that
   follows?

   _____

   _____

   _____

   _____

   _____

   _____

   _____

   _____

   _____

   _____

EXERCISE 32 **Adding your supporting details**

Write your topic sentence. Then list each key idea. Add supporting details to explain the key ideas in your topic sentence.

Topic sentence: _____

_____

A. Key Idea: _____

    1. Supporting Detail:

    _____

    2. Supporting Detail:

    _____

B. Key Idea: _____

    1. Supporting Detail:

    _____

    2. Supporting Detail:

    _____

C. Key Idea: _____

    1. Supporting Detail:

    _____

    2. Supporting Detail:

    _____

D. Key Idea: _____

    1. Supporting Detail:

    _____

    2. Supporting Detail:

    _____

EXERCISE 33 **Writing your concluding sentence**

Look at your topic sentence, your key ideas, and your supporting details. Then decide on an appropriate concluding sentence. Write it here:

_____

_____

_____

Writing, Editing, and Revising

EXERCISE 34 **Writing your draft paragraph**

Write your draft paragraph, using the Academic Format Standards.

EXERCISE 35 **Editing your draft paragraph**

Now check your writing. Can you say Yes for all four statements?

- I used the Academic Format Standards.
- I checked for sentence completeness.
- I checked for subject-verb agreement.
- I checked for parallel structures.

EXERCISE 36 **Doing a peer review**

Exchange paragraphs with a classmate and use Peer Review Form 3-2 in the appendix to give each other feedback on your work.

EXERCISE 37 **Revising your first draft**

Before you revise, ask yourself these questions:

- How can I use the peer review to improve my paragraph?
- How do I feel about this paragraph? Am I proud of it?
- Am I making progress in my academic writing?
- Is this the best work I can do?

Make any changes you think are necessary to your first draft. Keep working on the paragraph until you can answer Yes to the last question. Then rewrite the paragraph and turn it in to your instructor.

EXERCISE 38   **Practicing evaluating paragraphs**

In Exercise 29, you evaluated Marcella's topic sentence. Here is her complete paragraph. Read it now to understand her ideas about herself.

Student Sample 7

The Real Marcella

I am a person who can be very intelligent in a business, especially in a restaurant. I have worked in a restaurant since I graduated from high school. I can resolve most of the problems with the customers because I have a way to talk to them. I enjoy talking to people and exchanging ideas with them. I have always enjoyed interacting with people, from the time I first learned to talk. I also do my job really well, but I'm not very smart in books. I am not like those people who can sit down for hours and read one book because I feel sleepy. Since I was a child, I haven't liked quiet activities like reading for hours on end. I have never been a couch potato. I would love to be like those people who read different kinds of books every day. I do well in ESL class because I like to talk and participate, especially when I'm in groups where I can exchange ideas with other students and instructors.

Marcella

With a partner, do the following tasks:

1. Underline the topic sentence in Marcella's paragraph.
2. Her major points or key ideas are:

   ■ She can resolve most problems with customers because she has a way to talk to them.
   ■ She does her job well, but she's not very smart with books.

3. Draw a box around the supporting details that help illustrate or explain these major points or key ideas.
4. Would you like to ask Marcella questions, such as the name of the restaurant <u>where</u> she works? <u>What</u> kind of job she does there?
5. Is there an example of <u>how</u> she solved a problem with a customer? (Remember the five W and one H questions.)
6. Marcella needs a concluding sentence. Write one for her:

_____

_____

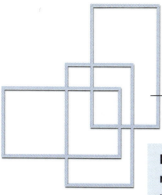

Writing Assignment 3

In this writing assignment, you will explain a decision you have made or will make. You will learn a logical process based on decision matrices to make that decision. First, you will gather information and learn about the technique.

⬚ Gathering Information

EXERCISE 39 **Making decisions**

Once you set a goal, you have to make decisions before you can proceed to that goal. How do you do that? Check any strategies you have used in making a decision:

_____ Consult my friends

_____ Read my horoscope

_____ Visit a psychic or a fortune teller

_____ Ask my mother

_____ Ask my father

_____ Ask my older brother or sister

_____ Ask my instructor or counselor

_____ Ask my girlfriend or boyfriend

_____ Roll dice

_____ Not make a decision and let fate decide for me

_____ Pray for guidance

_____ Flip a coin

_____ Do what my friends have done

_____ Do research in the library

_____ Do research on the World Wide Web

_____ Use a logical process

EXERCISE **40** **Discussing strategies with others**

In a small group, discuss your decision-making strategies.

■ Which strategies are used most often by your group? List them here:

_____

_____

_____

_____

_____

_____

■ Does anyone use the last strategy, Use a   Yes   No
logical process?

■ Does anyone know a logical process for   Yes   No
decision making?

Perhaps you circled No for the last two questions. As you prepare to write this paragraph assignment, you will learn about a logical process that

---

Terms You Need to Know

A *decision matrix** is a chart to help organize your thoughts.

■ First, you decide which factors or *criteria** are most important to you.

■ Then, you apply those factors or criteria to help make your choice.

<u>Criteria</u> is the plural form of <u>criterion</u>. A criterion is a standard rule on which a judgment or decision can be based. A <u>matrix</u> is a chart formed with columns and rows used to arrange ideas. The plural of <u>matrix</u> is <u>matrices</u>. Add these words to your Word Bank if you haven't already done so.

EXERCISE 41 Combining sentences to give reasons

First, you will learn about using a decision matrix to make a logical decision by working through the process with Andre. Then, you will combine sentences about Andre's information after you find out more about him. Read the following information about Andre.

Andre wants to get a bachelor's degree in international business. There are several universities in the area where he lives, and he wants to choose the best one for him. How does he do that? First, he decides what is most important to him in his decision. Each criterion has a reason.

Column A Criteria	Column B Reason for criteria
1. The university must have an international business major.	I want to major in international business.
2. The university must have a graduate program in international business.	I might decide to do graduate work in international business.
3. The university must be in my commuting area.	I want to live at home to save money.
4. The tuition should be reasonable.	My finances are limited.
5. The university should accept my community college credits.	I do not want to lose credits I have earned.

Combine the sentence in Column A with the sentence in Column B, the reason.

- You can use this pattern: SENTENCE A + BECAUSE + SENTENCE B.
- You can also use this pattern: SENTENCE B + , SO + SENTENCE A.

The connecting words *because* and *so* show the relationship between the two ideas. For example:

> a
1. **A.** The university must have an international business major **because**
>   b
   I want to major in international business.
>   b   a
   B. I want to major in international business, **so** the university must have an international business major.

Now do the rest of the sentences, combining each sentence in two ways. (Remember to use a comma before the word so.)

2. A. _____

   _____

   B. _____

   _____

3. A. _____

   _____

   B. _____

   _____

4. A. _____

   _____

   B. _____

   _____

5. A. _____

   _____

   B. _____

   _____

After you have written all eight sentences, ask a classmate to check them to make sure they are right. Do the same for your classmate.

EXERCISE 42   Rewriting because sentences

In Exercise 41, you used this pattern: SENTENCE A + BECAUSE + SENTENCE B.

For example, look at this sentence:

> The university must have an international business major **because** I want to major in international business.

Rewrite it now like this:

> **Because** I want to major in international business, the university must have an international business major.

Do you notice a change in the capitalization? What is it?

_____

Do you notice a change in the punctuation? What is it?

_____

- If you said that *because* becomes *Because* in the second sentence, you are right.
- If you said that a comma follows the *because* clause, you are right. When a clause begins with *because*, you follow the clause with a comma. (Do not put the comma right after *because*!)

Now rewrite all the sentences with the because *clause at the beginning. Don't forget the comma.*

1. **Because** _____

_____

2. **Because** _____

_____

3. **Because** _____

_____

4. **Because** _____

_____

EXERCISE 43 Studying Andre's Decision Matrix—Part A

Study how Andre completed his Decision Matrix—Part A. Then answer some questions.

a. First, Andre writes his criteria in the left-hand column of the matrix.
b. Next, he decides how important to him each criterion is. He gives more points to the important criteria.

Decision Matrix—Part A			
Criteria	Extremely important (3 points)	Very important (2 points)	Somewhat important (1 point)
1. University must have undergraduate degree in international business.	X		
2. University should offer graduate degree in international business.			X
3. University must be within commuting distance of my house so that I can live at home.	X		
4. Tuition should be reasonable (under $7,000 per year).		X	
5. University should accept my transfer credits from the community college.		X	

With a partner, answer these questions:

- How many criteria does Andre have? _____

- Which two criteria are the <u>most important</u> to him?

  _____

  and _____

- Which criterion is the <u>least important</u> to him?

  _____

  _____

  _____

- Which criteria are <u>very important</u> to Andre?

  _____

  _____

  _____

EXERCISE 44 **Studying Andre's Decision Matrix—Part B**

Now study how Andre uses Decision Matrix—Part B. Then answer the questions with your partner.

- He lists the three colleges he is considering at the top.
- He rates each one on the basis of his criteria.
- In other words, if a university meets a criterion, he gives it points:
  - "extremely important" is worth 3 points,
  - "very important" is worth 2 points, and
  - "somewhat important" is worth 1 point
- If a university does not meet a criterion, he gives it no points (0 points).
- He writes the number of points in each university's column.
- Finally, he adds up the points for each university and writes them in the last row.

Decision Matrix—Part B			
Criteria	University A	University B	University C
1. University must have undergraduate degree in international business. *Weight = 3*	3	3	3
2. University should offer graduate degree in international business. *Weight = 1*	1	0	1
3. University should be within commuting distance of my house so that I can live at home. *Weight = 3*	0	3	3
4. Tuition should be reasonable (under $7,000 per year). *Weight = 2*	2	2	0
5. University should accept my transfer credits from the community college. *Weight = 2*	2	2	0
TOTAL POINTS FOR EACH UNIVERSITY	8	10	7

With a partner, answer these questions:

- Which university does not offer a graduate degree in international business?

  _____

  _____

- Which university is not within commuting distance of Andre's home?

  _____

  _____

- Which university costs more than $7,000 for tuition?

  _____

  _____

- Which university will not accept his transfer credits from the community college?

  _____

  _____

- Which university gets the most points?

  _____

  _____

- Which university gets the fewest points?

  _____

  _____

- According to this decision process, which is the best university for Andre to attend? Circle the answer:

  University A   University B   University C

EXERCISE 45 **Giving Andre other possibilities**

Sometimes we do not choose the most logical option. Then we have to be creative and think of other ways to attain our goal. For example, let's say that Andre chooses University B to get his bachelor's degree. Then, after a year, he decides to study for a graduate degree in international business. University B does not have a graduate program in international business. What could he do? Write as many possibilities as you can think of for Andre:

1. (For example) <u>Andre could ask the department to start a graduate program in international business.</u>

2. _____

   _____

3. _____

   _____

4. _____

   _____

5. _____

   _____

6. _____

   _____

Compare your answers with your partner's. How many times did you use these words: could, may, might, *and* should? *They are helpful when we are writing about possibilities. Read the Power Grammar tip for more information.*

P O W E R   G R A M M A R

Using Vocabulary to Control the Tone of Your Writing

Academic writing uses a special style in the statement of ideas and information. Generally, academic writing is careful and does not make big claims. Generalizations are given with words that make the writer seem careful.

Academic writers have to be careful about facts. Usually, words like *all* and *none*, *always* and *never* are avoided because the statement is too general.

All high school students want to go to college. (Not true. *Many* do, but *some* don't.) *Students who study always pass.* (Not true, unfortunately. Students who study *usually* pass but sometimes fail.)

Words like *may* and *might* are often used to tone down a generalization. "Tone down" means to make a statement less strong.

People who have degrees in information technology may have more trouble finding jobs today than in the 1990s.

Could is also used for this purpose.

If you earn a PhD, you could earn more money than if you have only a master's degree.

Should can be advice that is less direct and less of a command than *must*.

You should study three hours for every hour you spend in class.

Words like *perhaps* are also used to tone down writing. (*Maybe* has the same meaning but is more conversational and less academic.)

Perhaps you should study more than you do now if you want to improve your grades.

EXERCISE 46   **Toning down language**

Tone down each of these statements by changing some of the words.

1. American teenagers never show respect to their instructors.

   _____

   _____

   _____

2. All people on welfare are lazy and refuse to work.

   _____

   _____

   _____

3. My college instructors are never fair in giving grades.

   _____

   _____

   _____

4. Politicians always lie to the public.

   _____

   _____

   _____

5. If I buy a lottery ticket every day, I will win the jackpot.

   _____

   _____

   _____

6. You failed the test because you didn't study.

   _____

   _____

   _____

EXERCISE 47 **Choosing a topic**

Remember that your writing assignment is to explain a decision you have made or will make, using the logical process based on Decision Matrix A and Decision Matrix B. You can use any decision for this assignment. The decision must involve some choices. Here are some possibilities. Check any that interest you. At the end of the list, add more ideas that you find especially interesting:

_____ Whether to buy a house, rent a house, or rent an apartment

_____ Whether to live at home with your parents or in a dormitory

_____ Whether to live with friends, with your sisters, or by yourself

_____ Whether to look for a new job or keep your old job

_____ Which job offer to accept

_____ Whether to buy a new car or a used car

_____ Which used car to buy

_____ Whether to be a full-time or a part-time student

_____ Whether to get married or stay single

_____ Whether to major in information technology, computer networking, or computer programming

_____

_____

_____

EXERCISE 48 **Freewriting about possible topic choices**

Select one to three topics from Exercise 47 and freewrite about each to decide which topic you will choose.

Then freewrite again for five minutes about the topic you have chosen. Write down as many ideas as you can on the decision you made, including these:

- your options or choices
- your criteria
- why the criteria are important

EXERCISE 49   Complete Decision Matrix—Part A

Now write your criteria in Decision Matrix—Part A below. Then use an X to indicate how important each criterion is to you. See Exercise 43 for an example.

Decision Matrix—Part A			
Criteria in my decision	**Extremely important (3)**	**Very important (2)**	**Somewhat important (1)**
1.			
2.			
3.			
4.			

EXERCISE 50   Completing Decision Matrix—Part B

Copy your criteria and your options (choices) in Decision Matrix—Part B. Then assign the weight for each criterion to each option. Add up the numbers for each option and write the total in the last row. See Exercise 44 for an example.

Decision Matrix—Part B			
Criteria in my decision	**Option A:**	**Option B:**	**Option C:**
1. *Weight =*			
2. *Weight =*			
3. *Weight =*			
4. *Weight =*			
Total points for each option			

🔲 Focusing and Organizing

EXERCISE 51 Focusing your ideas and add details

While looking at your Decision Matrix—Part B, answer these questions:

1. Which of your options seems the best, based on the total points?

2. Which seems second best?

3. Which seems worst?

EXERCISE 52 Showing your decision matrices to a partner

Show your Decision Matrix—Part A and Decision Matrix—Part B to a classmate and explain your decision. Answer any questions your partner may have about your decision, your criteria, your options, and the points you assigned to each option. Clear up any confusion. Then do the same for your partner.

EXERCISE 53 Writing your topic sentence

Write a topic sentence that states your decision and gives a reason for your decision.

My topic sentence:

_____

_____

_____

_____

_____

_____

EXERCISE 54 **Choosing a way to organize your paragraph**

There are two convenient ways to organize your paragraph. Study the following information and discuss it with other members of your class.

- Your criteria could be your major points. (Plan A)
- Or you could use each option as a major point. (Plan B)

Your supporting details will be organized by how you chose your major points. Andre, for example, tried both ways.

Plan A		Plan B	
Topic Sentence: University B is the best for me because it meets all my criteria.		Topic Sentence: After I compared University C, University A, and University B, I decided to choose University B for my undergraduate work.	
Major point	**Supporting details**	**Major point**	**Supporting details**
Most important to me is being able to study for an undergraduate degree in international business.	B has this major. C and A also offer this degree.	University C is lacking in some ways I think are important.	Tuition is $20,000 per year.
But I'm thinking about graduate work in that area, too.	B doesn't have this program, but I do not know if I would want to do graduate work anyway.		It won't accept my community college credits.
	A and C do have international business graduate programs.	University A meets some of my criteria.	But I would have to live on campus.
I want to live at home and commute.	Both B and C are close enough so that I could do this.		That would be expensive.

Plan A		Plan B	
Major point	**Supporting details**	**Major point**	**Supporting details**
	A is too far away. I would have to live on campus. I would miss my family.		I would miss my family.
I don't want to pay more than $7,000 in tuition each year.	A and B both charge less than that.	University B meets most of my criteria.	It has the right major, international business.
	C is too expensive.		It does not have a graduate program in the same field. But I may not want to continue studying— I don't know.
The university has to accept my community college credits so that I do not waste my money when I transfer.	A and B will accept them. C will not.		It has reasonable tuition.
			I can live at home and commute.
Concluding Sentence:		Concluding Sentence:	

How will you organize your paragraph?

_____ I will use each <u>criterion</u> as a major point. (Plan A)

_____ I will use each <u>option</u> as a major point. (Plan B)

EXERCISE 55   **Writing concluding sentences**

Write a concluding sentence for one of Andre's planned paragraphs (either Plan A or Plan B). Use the space in the plan marked Concluding sentence.

Then write your own concluding sentence that does one of these things:

- Restates your topic sentence
- Tells how you feel about your decision
- Predicts how your decision will affect your future
- Leaves the reader with a thought about the decision-making process

Your concluding sentence: _____

_____

Writing, Editing, and Revising

EXERCISE 56   **Drafting your paragraph**

Now you are ready to write the first draft of your paragraph. You may wish to have your decision matrices in front of you as you write.

EXERCISE 57   **Editing your paragraph**

Check your work carefully for these four points. Add two more editing problems you will check your writing for.

- Did you use Academic Format Standards?   Yes   No

- Is each sentence complete?   Yes   No

- Are all sentences beginning with *Because*   Yes   No
  punctuated correctly?

- Did you use parallel structures?   Yes   No

- _____?   Yes   No

- _____?   Yes   No

EXERCISE 58 Doing a read-around peer review

Sit in a group with other students who wrote on a topic similar to yours. In other words, all students who wrote on a career decision should sit in a circle. All students who wrote on an academic decision should form another circle, and so on.

Attach your paragraph to your Decision Matrix—Part A and Decision Matrix—Part B. Write your name at the top of Read-Around Peer Review Form 3-3 in the appendix.

Give your paragraph (with matrices attached) and your Read-Around Peer Review Form to the person at your right. That person initials on the left side of question 1, writes an answer, and passes the paper on to the next student, who initials on the left of question 2 and writes an answer to it. Keep doing this until all of the questions on the Read-Around Peer Review Form 3-3 have been answered.

Get your paragraph, matrices, and Read-Around Peer Review Form 3-3 back from the last person who read your paragraph.

EXERCISE 59 Revising your paragraph

Consider the comments made by your group of peer reviewers. Then make any changes you think are needed for your paragraph. List three changes here that you plan to make:

1. _____

2. _____

3. _____

When you are confident that it is your best work, rewrite your paragraph. Attach both matrices and the Read-Around Peer Review Form 3-3. Give it to your instructor.

⬚ Additional Topics for More Practice and Assessment

- Describe one useful skill you learned in Chapter 3. Be specific. Tell how you will use that skill in the future.
- Does the logical process for making decisions that you practiced in Writing Assignment 3 seem like a useful tool for you? Why or why not?
- Could you use the decision-making matrices to convince your wife or husband or parents that a choice you want to make is a good one?
- In your opinion, do a person's decisions determine what happens to her or him in life, or does fate or destiny play a more important role?
- Describe the most difficult decision you ever made in your life. Tell how you made the decision.
- Many American parents tell their children, "You can be anything you want to be." Do you believe that what the parents say is true, or are they deceiving their children?
- Do you know a proverb or a saying about goals and decisions? Write about it. Discuss whether you think it is true. (For example, A trip of a thousand miles begins with a single step.)
- Sometimes people think they have no choices in life. Have you ever felt that way? Explain.

⬚ Reflection on Chapter 3

EXERCISE 60   **Self-evaluating**

Chapter 3 Academic Writing Objectives were the following:

- Distinguish between general and specific details
- Use infinitives, check for parallel structure
- Control the tone of your writing
- Write more powerful sentences

All of these goals have one purpose: To help you write academic English so that you can succeed in the college classroom. *How do you feel about your progress toward good academic writing at this point? When you have completed these sentences, give a copy of them to your instructor.*

1. I feel very confident / somewhat confident / not at all confident about my progress.

2. I have the most progress in _____.

3. I have made the least progress in _____.

4. I now enjoy writing more / less than I did at the beginning of the

   term because _____

   _____.

5. I need a lot more work in _____.

6. I could help other students in _____
   because I am good in that area.

7. My vocabulary is _____.

8. I am happiest about _____.

9. And, finally, _____

   _____

   _____.

W E B   P O W E R

A final word: Do you want more practice on any grammar points in Chapter 3? You will find additional exercises related to the content in this chapter at
http://esl.college.hmco.com/students·

Balancing Responsibilities

Academic Writing Objectives

- Persuade and give advice through writing
- Explore both sides of an issue
- Respond to a case study
- Review count/noncount nouns; control tone using modals; relate time using past, present, and present perfect tenses

Here is what to expect in this chapter:

You will write a paragraph on →	For the purpose of →	Focus on these writing skills →	Learn this Power Grammar →	Use these graphic organizers →	With this vocabulary focus
How you manage your time to meet your responsibilities	Description	More work on examples and details Effective topic sentences, concluding sentences	Count and noncount nouns	Mind map Outline Peer review form	"Advice" as a noncount noun
One thing you worry about	Description	Details and examples			Develop your own definitions
Advice to a student with a dilemma	Problem/ solution Persuasion	Appropriate tone	Control tone of writing (modals)	Social letter format	Choose appropriate language More words to control tone
Pros and cons of credit cards	Analysis Problem/ solution	General vs. specific Analysis of pros and cons Strong reasons		Peer review	Vocabulary of taking sides
Advice based on a case study	Analysis Problem/ solution Persuasion	Analysis and application	Present perfect in academic writing	Timeline Life list	

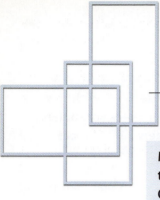

Writing Assignment 1

Many college students are more than just students. In addition to their college classes, some students have family responsibilities. Others have a job to help pay their college expenses and to support themselves. For this writing assignment, you will write a paragraph explaining how you manage your time to meet all your responsibilities. You will be specific and give examples to illustrate your ideas.

EXERCISE 1 **Discussing your secrets for success**

*With a partner, discuss how you balance everything you have to do with your role as a student. What advice would you give another student who wants to be a successful student but has many other responsibilities? Write two pieces of **advice*** to other students on how to balance responsibilities. If possible, tell ideas that have worked successfully for you:*

_____

_____

Advice

Did you notice that Exercise 1 asks you to write "two pieces of advice"? *Advice* is not a noun that can be counted.

You cannot say ~~two advices~~ or ~~an advice~~.

> You *can* say: He gave me <u>advice</u>.
> He gave me <u>some advice</u>.
> He gave me a <u>piece of advice</u>.
> He gave me <u>lots of advice</u>.

Add the above phrases to your Word Bank in the appendix. Read more about similar "noncount" nouns in the Power Grammar tip.

POWER GRAMMAR

Count and Noncount Nouns

In academic writing, it is important to know whether you are using a count noun or a noncount noun so that you form the plural correctly and know how to use it.

	Singular	Plural
Count nouns have singular and plural forms. Regular plural nouns add -*s* or -*es* to the singular form.	job	jobs
	class	class**es**
Count nouns that are *irregular* form plurals in different ways. You can find the spellings in the dictionary.	man	men
	criterion	criteria
	matrix	matrices
Noncount nouns do not have different singular or plural forms.	advice	Yes
	~~An advice~~	No
	~~Two advices~~	No

There are clues to help you decide if a noun is noncount. Many noncount nouns are:

1. things that come in very small pieces: — *rice, salt, sand*

2. wholes made up of similar parts (but the parts are often count nouns): — *food, furniture, luggage*

3. names of subjects of study: — *ESL, biology, mathematics*

4. abstractions (general ideas): — *happiness, justice, luck*

5. liquids/fluids: — *blood, milk, water*

6. gases: — *carbon monoxide, oxygen, hydrogen*

7. solids/minerals: — *gold, ice, mercury*

8. sports/types of recreation: — *chess, tennis, soccer*

9. natural phenomena (things that exist in nature): — *dew, rain, snow*

10. diseases: — *measles, mumps, smallpox*

You cannot use *a* or *an* with noncount nouns.	~~I gave her an advice.~~	No
	~~I gave her two advices.~~	No
	I gave her a piece of advice.	Yes
However, you can put words in front that mean more than one.	*I gave her some advice.*	Yes
	I have gotten lots of advice from my family.	Yes

(Continued)

Some nouns can be both count and noncount words, but their meanings are different. The noncount version is about a general area; the count versions are pieces or units of the larger area.

Noncount
Fashion *is a waste of time.*

Count
*She wore **a fashion** from the 1960s.*
Cake *is usually served at birthday parties in our family. We all really like **cake.***
*I bought **a cake** for my sister's party. We had **three cakes** at her party.*

Check Your Dictionary
Your dictionary will tell you with a symbol if a noun is noncount. Often ***U*** is used to mean ***uncountable*** (in other words, *noncount*).

EXERCISE **2** **Adding other noncount nouns**

Work with another student. Add words to each of these groups. Then check your answers by using a dictionary that labels noncount nouns.

1. things that come in very small pieces:	*rice, salt, sand,*
2. wholes made up of similar parts (but the parts are often count nouns):	*food, furniture, luggage,*
3. names of subjects of study:	*ESL, biology, mathematics,*
4. abstractions (general ideas):	*happiness, justice, luck,*
5. liquids/fluids:	*blood, milk, water,*

6. gases:	carbon monoxide, oxygen, hydrogen,
7. solids/minerals:	gold, ice, mercury,
8. sports/types of recreation:	chess, tennis, soccer,
9. natural phenomena (things that exist in nature):	dew, rain, snow,
10. diseases:	measles, mumps, smallpox,

EXERCISE 3   Making sentences with noncount nouns

Write a sentence using a noncount noun from the group in Exercise 2.
For example, diseases*:*

1. (diseases) As a child, I had malaria_____.

2. (sports) _____

3. (natural phenomena) _____

4. (names of subjects of study) _____

5. (things that come in small pieces) _____

6. (gases) _____

7. (things that come in very small pieces) _____

8. (liquids) _____

Ask another student to look at your sentences and check them to be sure
that your noncount nouns:

- do not end in *-s* for plural meaning.
- do not have **a** or **an** in front of them (but they may have a phrase
   such as **some** or **lots of** in front of them).

If the student is not sure about your sentences, ask your instructor for help.

EXERCISE 4   Reading what other students said

Here is what some students said about balancing their responsibilities. Read carefully to see how different students write about this topic. Then, answer the questions in Exercise 5.

Student Sample 1 (Sung Shic)

We have to manage our time so that we can do everything we need to do. In my country, Korea, most students don't have a job because parents support their sons or daughters and pay their school tuition. In America I was surprised that many students have a part-time or full-time job. Most people in my class went to work after school. I got a part-time job, but then I didn't have time to do homework. I made a schedule for my day and for my week, but I needed more time to study, so I reduced my sleeping. For example, I need at least seven hours a day to sleep, but I reduced it by two hours so that I would have enough time to study. One week later, I could not do that anymore because it was too difficult. I was very tired and sleepy. Right now I have found a good schedule for me. My plan is that I go to bed early and wake up early, so although I sleep only seven hours, I can study early when my mind is awake. It is hard to do, but it is important because if you make your schedule, you may know if you waste time each day or week, and then you might be able to save that time.

Sung Shic

Student Sample 2 (Labiba)

Time is a precious thing, so we should take advantage of every single second. There are many ways to save time. It sounds impossible, but we can make it possible. When I came to the United States, I got more responsibilities. I didn't know how to manage them. I thought the time was flying here. I wasn't sure of performing my duties perfectly and on time, for the time was too limited. Now I realize that I am successful. The main reason for my success is my hard work to save time. First, I never put off today's work for tomorrow. I make a schedule for my daily activities, and I concentrate on one thing at a time. I am patient and disciplined while performing my duties. I recommend that you, too, follow these steps in order to be successful.

Labiba

Student Sample 3 (Robel)

If we manage our time, we will improve our standard of living. We have to make plans for study, for work, and for recreation. Even if we don't have enough time, we have to use every second on important things. We must not waste our time by drinking coffee. Actually, I have had a problem in managing my time, but now I have learned from my experience. If we use every minute in working or studying, our life will change. But if we waste our entire time in the wrong places like nightclubs and in drinking, we will never improve our life. We have to manage our time to be successful in our daily life. There is nothing impossible in our world if we work hard and manage our time. Planning helps us do on time everything that we need to do.

Robel

Student Sample 4 (Sedigheh)

In my opinion, we never find enough time to do everything that we like to do, but if we make an organized program, it can help us to do almost everything that we are supposed to do. Sometimes we might get dizzy from all of the things that we want to do. It would be possible if a day was 48 or 72 hours long and we just needed to sleep 7 hours a day. Unfortunately, it is impossible when we have only 24 hours a day. So the best way is to think which is the most important thing to do, and do it first. For example, before I started ESL class, I just spent time doing nothing, like waking up late in the morning and watching TV a lot. I was losing a lot of time without doing anything important for my life. When I had something to do that was important, I left it for later. Then I started school. It is hard, but I am a lot happier because I think I am using my time well and I am doing something for my future.

Sedigheh

Student Sample 5 (Yahya)

Most people think that they don't have enough time, but I don't agree with them because everyone has the same amount and many people can do a lot of work in the same amount of time without complaining about it. So we can do everything we need if we manage our time. There are many examples to show how managing our time makes us successful. My boss manages his time well. He starts his day at 5 a.m. with exercise, then eats breakfast, reads the newspaper, and watches TV. He arrives at his office before anyone else. He does all his activities on time, and he doesn't delay any work for tomorrow. He writes his report immediately after finishing his work. I can say I manage my time well because I'm a student, and I have a full-time job and a family to take care of; however, I have free time, too, because I plan my time. Finally, everyone can do everything he needs if he manages his time but is not lazy or unwilling. I have advice:

1. Don't delay today's work until tomorrow because tomorrow has its own work.

2. Don't take a rest before finishing your duty.

3. You must be on time.

4. Don't wait for others to do your homework.

5. Write down everything you need to do.

6. Begin with important things you have to do.

Yahya

EXERCISE 5   **Answering questions about paragraphs**

Work with a partner, and answer these questions:

1. Which students use <u>specific examples</u> of how <u>they themselves</u>

   manage their time? _____

   ▪ Put brackets [ ] around specific examples in two students'
     paragraphs.

2. Some students use <u>other people's ideas</u> on how to manage time.

   For example, Yahya tells how _____

   manages time well.

3. Some students talk about the topic in general terms but <u>don't give</u>
   <u>many details</u> to illustrate their ideas.

   ▪ For example, do you wonder what kind of job Sung Shic had? What
     are some other questions you would like to ask him?

   _____

   _____

   ▪ Also, do you know if Labiba has a job? Family responsibilities?

   _____

   ▪ Does Sedigheh tell you if she has a job or family?

   _____

4. Which student <u>compares</u> the life of students in his own country with
   the life of students in the United States?

   _____

5. Which student <u>compares</u> life <u>before</u> starting classes with life <u>now</u>?

   _____

6. Which student's paragraph do you like the best? _____

   Why do you prefer it to the others? _____

   _____

☐ Focusing and Organizing Information

EXERCISE 6   Reading a mind map

An excellent way to gather your thoughts before you write is to make a
mind map.* This is a diagram that shows what you are thinking. Here is
a mind map of one student's responsibilities.

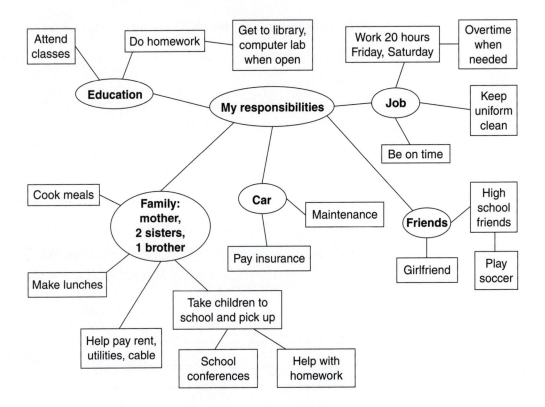

*Notice how the student wrote "My responsibilities" in the center. What
major kinds of responsibilities does he have? Fill in the blanks:*

   Education   _____   _____   _____

_____

*The lines and boxes attached to each oval shape show the details about each
responsibility. For example, look at the oval shape for his job. Answer these
questions:*

■ How many hours per week does he work? _____

- Which days does he work? _____

- Does he work overtime? _____

- He seems to be concerned about two details. What are they?

1. _____

2. _____

EXERCISE 7   Adding details by asking questions

What are some questions you would want to ask the student who made the mind map in Exercise 6? With a classmate, make a list of questions (who, what, when, where, why, and how—the Five Ws and 1 H you learned about in Chapter 3).

_____

_____

_____

EXERCISE 8   Making a mind map of your responsibilities

Try making a mind map of your responsibilities. Put all your ideas into it, and attach examples and details to the major categories of responsibilities.

Show your mind map to a classmate. Answer her or his questions (who, what, when, where, why, and how) to clarify your mind map and identify details you might want to add to it. You will use this mind map to help you plan your draft paragraph.

SPOTLIGHT ON WRITING SKILLS

The Topic Sentence

The topic sentence should be a general statement about how you manage all the responsibilities you have. It is a kind of *introduction* to the reader about the next information.

Do this exercise with a partner.

- *First reread the student samples in Exercise 4.*
- *Then look at the first sentences (below) and decide whether in the body of the paragraph the writer did what the topic sentence promised.*
- *The first two samples have been completed for you.* (Hint: *Answer* No *to only one of the last three paragraphs.*)

> **Sung Shic:** We have to manage our time so that we can do everything we need to do.

- What does Sung Shic do in his first two sentences? *He makes a general statement that we have to manage our time so that we can do what we have to do. Now we expect that he will tell us how he manages his time or how we should manage our time. Does he follow through in his paragraph?*

    __X__ Yes _____ No (Yes, he tells us about how he adjusted his schedule twice to get enough time to sleep and to study.)

> **Labiba:** Time is a precious thing, so we should take advantage of every single second.

- What does Labiba do in her first two sentences? *She makes a general statement about making the most of our time. We expect her to tell us how. Does she?*

    __X__ Yes _____ No (Yes, she gives four examples of how she makes the most of her time and recommends we use them.)

> **Robel:** If we manage our time, we will improve our standard of living.

- What does Robel do in his first two sentences? *He tells us that if we manage our time, we will have a better standard of living. Does he follow through in his paragraph?*

    _____ Yes _____No

Sedigheh: In my opinion, we never find enough time to do everything that we like to do, but if we make an organized program, it can help us to do almost everything that we are supposed to do.

▧ What does Sedigheh do in her sentence? *She tells us that an organized program or plan will help us do almost everything we are supposed to do, but not everything that we would like to do. Does Sedigheh's paragraph do what she promises to do?*

_____ Yes _____ No

Yahya: Most people think that they don't have enough time, but I don't agree with them because everyone has the same amount, and many people can do a lot of work in the same amount of time without complaining about it.

▧ What does Yahya do in his sentence? *He tells us that many people do more work than others in the same amount of time, and they do not complain about the lack of time. Does Yahya explain this in the rest of his paragraph?*

_____ Yes _____ No

Talk with another group about your answers. Do they agree or disagree? Are their *reasons* for agreeing or disagreeing the same as yours?

EXERCISE 10 **Evaluating topic sentences**

Which of these might be a good topic sentence for the student whose mind map is in Exercise 8? Check the one or two that you like best. Be ready to explain why you chose it. Cross out any that you think would not work to focus the paragraph or are not effective.

_____ **1.** My biggest responsibility is my family.

_____ **2.** When I look at all my responsibilities, I wonder how I do everything in just twenty-four hours a day.

_____ **3.** I successfully juggle my education, job, family, friends, and car by planning my time right down to the minute.

_____ **4.** I am Superman!

_____ **5.** Deciding what is important is the key to managing all of my responsibilities.

_____ **6.** I have responsibilities.

_____ **7.** My car insurance is too high.

_____ **8.** I have a mother, two sisters, and a brother.

Discuss your choices with other students.

EXERCISE 11 **Thinking about your topic sentence**

To plan your topic sentence, you should:

- *Review the assignment to be sure you understand the topic.*
- *Look at your mind map and decide on <u>a main idea that tells how you manage all your responsibilities</u>. It will be the focus for your entire paragraph. Remember, the paragraph must do what the topic sentence promises.*

Write your main idea here: _____

_____

EXERCISE 12 **Writing your topic sentence**

Write your topic sentence about how you successfully manage your responsibilities.

Topic sentence:

_____

_____

_____

Ask a classmate these questions:

1. What would you expect to follow this topic sentence in my paragraph?

Write your classmate's answer here:

_____

_____

_____

_____

_____

2. How could my topic sentence be more effective?

_____

_____

_____

_____

_____

_____

You may want to change your topic sentence if your classmate's expectations are different from what you plan to write about or if your sentence is not effective.

EXERCISE 13 **Discussing Labiba's outline**

Before you begin to write your draft paragraph, it is important to organize your ideas and details. Look at Labiba's outline below to see how she organized her draft paragraph.

Labiba's topic sentence: Time is a precious thing, so we should take advantage of every single second.

Labiba's Major Points and Supporting Details

A. [Major Point] There are many ways to save time.

   1. [supporting detail] It sounds impossible, but we can make it possible.

B. [Major Point] When I came to the United States, I got more responsibilities.

   1. [supporting detail] I didn't know how to manage them.

   2. [supporting detail] I thought time was flying.

   3. [supporting detail] I wasn't sure of performing my duties perfectly and on time.

   4. [supporting detail] Time was too limited.

C. [Major Point] Now I realize that I am successful. The main reason for my success is my hard work to save time.

   1. [supporting detail] I never put off today's work for tomorrow.

   2. [supporting detail] I made a schedule for my daily activities.

   3. [supporting detail] I concentrate on one thing at a time.

   4. [supporting detail] I am patient and disciplined while performing my duties.

[Conclusion] I recommend that you, too, follow these steps in order to be successful.

EXERCISE 14 **Organizing your paragraph**

From your mind map, choose the major points that will best support your topic sentence.

■ Major points could be different areas of responsibility you have.
■ Or they could be different ways in which you have managed to balance your responsibilities.

It depends on your topic sentence.

Complete the outline with your major points and supporting details.
Use your mind map.

Topic sentence:

_____

_____

Major points and supporting details (*Note:* You may have fewer major points and more details.)

A. [Major Point] _____

   1. [supporting detail] _____

   2. [supporting detail] _____

B. [Major Point] _____

   1. [supporting detail] _____

   2. [supporting detail] _____

C. [Major Point] _____

   1. [supporting detail] _____

   2. [supporting detail] _____

D. [Major Point] _____

   1. [supporting detail] _____

   2. [supporting detail] _____

EXERCISE 15   **Finding what each concluding sentence does**

The concluding sentence is important because it is the last chance you have to leave a thought with the reader. You have learned four ways to end your paragraph. Notice that a fifth has been added: *A concluding sentence may also express a hopeful thought or inspirational idea.*

With a partner, look at the concluding sentences for these student samples. Check what each does: (Sung Shic's has been completed for you.)

> **Sung Shic:** [Sticking with a plan or schedule] is hard to do, but it is important because if you make your schedule, you may know if you waste time each day or week, and then you might be able to save that time.

_____ Summarize the main idea.

_____ Make a recommendation or give advice.

_____ Ask a question.

__X__ Make a prediction.

_____ Express a hopeful thought or inspirational idea.

> **Labiba:** I recommend that you, too, follow these steps in order to be successful.

_____ Summarize the main idea.

_____ Make a recommendation or give advice.

_____ Ask a question.

_____ Make a prediction.

_____ Express a hopeful thought or inspirational idea.

> **Robel:** Planning helps us do on time everything that we need to do.

_____ Summarize the main idea.

_____ Make a recommendation or give advice.

_____ Ask a question.

_____ Make a prediction.

_____ Express a hopeful thought or inspirational idea.

Sedigheh: [Going to school] is hard, but I am a lot happier because I think I am using my time and I am doing something for my future.

_____ Summarize the main idea.

_____ Make a recommendation or give advice.

_____ Ask a question.

_____ Make a prediction.

_____ Express a hopeful thought or inspirational idea.

Yahya: I have advice:

1. Don't delay today's work until tomorrow because tomorrow has its own work.

2. Don't take a rest before finishing your duty.

3. You must be on time.

4. Don't wait for others to do your homework.

5. Write down everything you need to do.

6. Begin with the important things you have to do.

_____ Summarize the main idea.

_____ Make a recommendation or give advice.

_____ Ask a question.

_____ Make a prediction.

_____ Express a hopeful thought or inspirational idea.

EXERCISE 16 **Writing your concluding sentence**

Now read what you have written, and decide on a concluding sentence that is appropriate for your paragraph. Write your concluding sentence here:

_____

_____

What does your concluding sentence do?

_____ Summarize the main idea.

_____ Make a recommendation or give advice.

_____ Ask a question.

_____ Make a prediction.

_____ Express a hopeful thought or inspirational idea.

▭ Writing, Editing, and Revising

EXERCISE 17 **Writing your paragaraph**

After you write your first draft, check it for:

- Academic Format Standards
- Complete sentences
- Subject-verb agreement
- Correct tense

EXERCISE 18 **Doing a peer review**

Exchange paragraphs with a classmate and use Peer Review Form 4-1 in the appendix to give each other feedback on your work.

EXERCISE 19 **Revising your paragraph**

Ask yourself these questions:

- How can I use my classmate's comments to improve my paragraph?
- Is this the best work I can do?

Then revise. Keep working on the paragraph until you can say you are proud of your work. Then turn the draft in to your instructor.

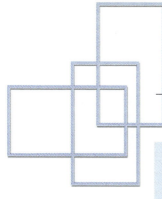

Writing Assignment 2

You have written about how you manage your responsibilities. Now, write a paragraph describing <u>one</u> thing you worry about as you balance your responsibilities as a student with other parts of your life.

This is an independent writing assignment. Follow the process you have been using: Gathering Information; Focusing and Organizing; Writing, Editing, and Revising.

EXERCISE 20 Understanding the assignment

Before you begin, see if you understand what you are to do. Select the correct answers:

1. I am going to write a paragraph / a sentence / an essay.
2. I will do it by myself / with a partner / with a small group / with the entire class.
3. I must follow a one-step process / two-step process / three-step process.
4. The topic is one thing I worry about as a student / two things I worry about in my social life / one thing most students worry about / my worries about life in general / what I worried about in high school.
5. This assignment is due _____.
6. My instructor wants / does not want me to develop an outline or mind map or other *graphic organizer** to show my plan.
7. I can / cannot ask my friends, classmates, or parents to help me with my writing.
8. I can / cannot ask a tutor to help me with my writing.

For statements 1–4, check your answers by rereading the assignment. For statements 5–8, talk to your instructor. Ask any questions you may have.

Developing Your Own Definition

In Exercise 20, an asterisk followed the term *graphic organizer*. This term may be unfamiliar to you and difficult to find in the dictionary. Here are some examples of graphic organizers you have used in this book:

- A Venn diagram
- An outline
- A mind map
- A matrix
- A chart

EXERCISE **21**   **Writing your own definition**

Work with another student. Use the examples above and on the dictionary definitions of graphic *and* organizer *to help you write your own definition of graphic organizer:*

_____

_____

_____

_____

_____

_____

Compare your definition with other students' definitions. Can you think of other examples of graphic organizers you have used?

_____

_____

_____

_____

_____

_____

Add your definition of graphic organizer *to your Word Bank in the appendix.*

EXERCISE 22 Looking at a student sample

Javier had the same assignment as you. Read what he wrote about his greatest worry.

Student Sample 6 (Javier)

Like any other person, I have my own worries. But my biggest worry involves my parents. I worry about my parents because they work too much. I don't want to see my parents working any more. I would like to see them enjoying the life they deserve. My father has two jobs and my mom has one job, but she also has to take care of my sister and the house, so that is like a second job for her. I am tired of seeing my parents' life just flying by. I don't see the day in which they are going to stop work and start to enjoy the beauty of life. In order for that to happen, I have to get a good education so that with the money I earn, it will be enough for my parents and me. In conclusion, my parents still are working hard for my older brothers, my sister, and me, and that will continue for a few more years. Perhaps someday in the future, they will be enjoying a life that they have always deserved.

Javier

EXERCISE 23 Ask questions to get more details

What are the questions you would like to ask Javier to understand his problem better? List them here. After you have finished your list, compare your questions with those of your classmates.

1. _____

2. _____

3. _____

4. _____

5. _____

EXERCISE **24** **Reading Javier's revised paragraph**

*When Javier revised his paragraph, he added more details (**bold print**) to his draft. His topic sentence is <u>underlined</u>. His main supporting points are italicized. Read his revised paragraph, and then answer the questions below the paragraph.*

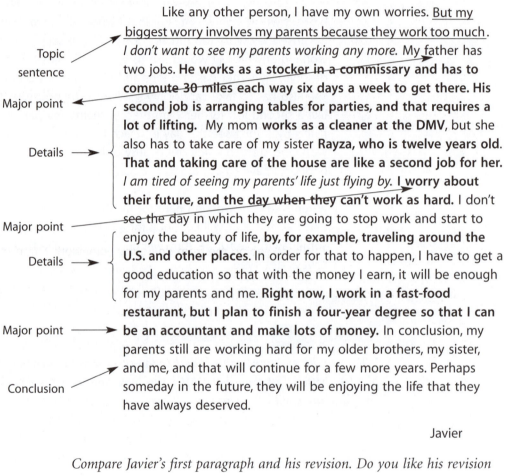

Topic sentence

Major point

Details

Major point

Details

Major point

Conclusion

Like any other person, I have my own worries. <u>But my biggest worry involves my parents because they work too much</u>. *I don't want to see my parents working any more.* My father has two jobs. **He works as a stocker in a commissary and has to commute 30 miles each way six days a week to get there. His second job is arranging tables for parties, and that requires a lot of lifting.** My mom **works as a cleaner at the DMV**, but she also has to take care of my sister **Rayza, who is twelve years old. That and taking care of the house are like a second job for her.** *I am tired of seeing my parents' life just flying by.* **I worry about their future, and the** day when they can't work as hard. I don't see the day in which they are going to stop work and start to enjoy the beauty of life, **by, for example, traveling around the U.S. and other places.** In order for that to happen, I have to get a good education so that with the money I earn, it will be enough for my parents and me. **Right now, I work in a fast-food restaurant, but I plan to finish a four-year degree so that I can be an accountant and make lots of money.** In conclusion, my parents still are working hard for my older brothers, my sister, and me, and that will continue for a few more years. Perhaps someday in the future, they will be enjoying the life that they have always deserved.

Javier

Compare Javier's first paragraph and his revision. Do you like his revision with added details better than his first draft?   Yes _____   No _____

Most people would answer Yes. Details help bring writing to life for the reader.

Writing Assignment 3

Sometimes students have a *dilemma** while trying to take care of all their responsibilities. A dilemma is a situation in which a person has to make a difficult choice between two options. For example, Marcella wrote about her dilemma in this paragraph. Your assignment is to write a letter to Marcella, showing her that you understand her dilemma and suggesting possible solutions. You will receive more details about the assignment when you get to the Focusing and Organizing step of the writing process.

Gathering Information

Student Sample 7 (Marcella)

I'm a hostess in a seafood restaurant, and I love my work. But it is keeping me from doing my homework. Often the manager asks me to stay late and help close the restaurant. I have worked at this restaurant for four years, and he has often asked me to do this. Until recently, I didn't mind because I wanted to show I was a hardworking, dedicated employee. Also, I need the money I earn at the restaurant to pay for my college tuition. But I hadn't realized that now I would need so much time to finish my homework. College is definitely not like high school! Now, when I have to stay late and help out when other employees are sick, I can't get my homework done, or I can't study for a test. Getting an associate's degree in restaurant management is my goal. This is confusing because I like my job but it is interfering with my long-term goal, to get an AA degree so that I can get my dream job, managing a really good restaurant. I don't know what to do.

Marcella

EXERCISE 25 Identifying Marcella's dilemma

What is the dilemma that Marcella has? Write two choices or options in this box:

Choice 1	Choice 2

EXERCISE 26 Thinking about a dilemma you have had

Write in the boxes your choices in a dilemma you have faced. (There may be more than two choices.) With a small group of students, discuss your dilemma. Explain what your decision was. (Another way to say this is how you solved your dilemma.)

Choice 1	Choice 2	Choice 3	Choice 4

How I solved my dilemma:

EXERCISE 27 Practicing dilemma solving

Here is more practice in dilemma solving. Choose two situations, and write some advice for each student. Be sure to write complete sentences that are punctuated correctly.

- Eun has an ESL class from 8:00 to 10:00 a.m. each weekday. She just received a telephone call asking her to come for a job interview tomorrow (Wednesday) at 8:30. What should Eun do?

_____

_____

_____

- Namib has already missed as many classes as he is allowed, because of health problems. His mother is arriving today for a three-week visit with Namib, her only son. She speaks no English and expects him to be with her twenty-four hours a day while she is here. What should Namib do?

_____

_____

_____

- Koffi just got a speeding ticket. He wants to go to court to fight the charge of speeding, but the court date is a day that his boss at Fairways Foods wants him to work as a cashier. What should Koffi do?

_____

_____

_____

- Susie's best friend, Maura, did not finish her writing assignment. Maura is in a different class but has received the same assignment that Susie got because they are at the same level. Maura asks Susie to let her copy the assignment. What should Susie do?

_____

_____

_____

▭ Focusing and Organizing

EXERCISE **28**   **Choosing words to suggest and give advice**

Study the vocabulary in the Power Grammar to help you choose words to advise Marcella about her dilemma. The words you use to give her advice must be carefully chosen.

POWER GRAMMAR

Controlling the Tone of Your Writing (Modals)

In Chapter 3, you learned about the importance of controlling your tone in academic writing. When you write to give advice, you need to be careful to use an appropriate tone to convince your reader to take your advice.

Commands are easy to write. But they are often not easy for people to accept. You have to have a special relationship with a person to give orders.

Example of a command:
Work fewer hours. [Too strong for advice.]
Get a loan. [Too strong for advice.]

Must and *have to* are also very strong words. They can only be used by a person who has power over another person. You can use these words to explain laws and requirements.

*At our college, students **must** (or **have to**) complete ESL before they can take freshman composition.* [This is all right if stated by a counselor or someone with authority at the college.]

You should probably avoid using *must* and *have to* when you are giving your own opinions and your advice. You probably do not have the power to make the reader take your advice. These examples are very strong and might offend your readers.

*You **must** quit your job.* [Too strong for advice.]

*You **have to** work fewer hours.* [Too strong for advice.]

(Continued)

Should is another useful word that can be tricky in writing. The meaning of *should* changes, depending on the source of the advice. This example simply reports the opinion of another person.

My adviser says that all students **should** take psychology classes to learn about human behavior.

Should means that the writer believes in the advice in a very strong way. The advice is based on the values and beliefs of the writer. You can present your values and beliefs but need to be aware of the possible negative reactions of readers.

I am a vegetarian. I believe that people **should** not eat animals. We **should** only eat vegetables. We **should** never eat anything that causes the death of another living creature.

I am studying nutrition. I have learned that we **should** change our diets to eat more vegetables. We **should** eat less meat and more vegetables and grains. If we make this change, we will be healthier.

Ought to is another way to say *should*. It is usually too strong for giving advice.

You **ought to** change your schedule and work fewer hours. [Too strong]

In academic writing, writers usually need to be less direct in giving advice. Your readers will be happier to get polite advice rather than strong commands. Modals such as *might* and *could* (or *can*) are less direct. This means the writer gives the reader a choice. The writer is not acting "bossy."

You **might** try working fewer hours.

You **could** try working fewer hours.

You **can** try working fewer hours.

Words like *can, could, should, ought to, may,* and *might* are called "modals". The verb that follows the modal is always in its simple form. Do not change it (for example, to its past tense form or plural form).

Correct
She **might try** working less.

Incorrect
She ~~**might tries** working less.~~

EXERCISE 29 **Trying out some words to make suggestions**

Use at least <u>three</u> of these verbs to make suggestions for Marcella:
should, could, can, might. *Try to use the ones you usually don't use when you speak.*

1. Example: <u>You might consider quitting your job and getting a</u>
<u>loan from the bank to cover your tuition.</u>

2. _____

3. _____

4. _____

5. _____

EXERCISE 30 **Role playing: How practical is your advice?**

In a small group of students, explain the advice you wrote in Exercise 29. Ask your group whether your advice seems practical. In other words, is it likely to work?

A. *First, choose one person to be Marcella.*

B. *Then, tell "Marcella" what you think she should do.*

C. *Marcella will respond to your advice.*

D. *The other students in the group can offer their suggestions.*

For example:

You: You should consider quitting your job and getting a loan from the bank to cover your tuition.

Marcella: How could I do that? I haven't built up my credit, and I think banks require a good credit rating before they lend money to people.

Student A: Some banks are willing to give loans at higher interest rates if you haven't built up your credit yet.

Student B: Or you could try getting a student loan. Go to the Financial Aid Office and ask the counselors there.

Marcella: I am not a citizen. I only have a green card. I'm not sure I can get a student loan.

You: The counselors in the financial aid office can tell you what your loan options are.

Student B: Maybe you could work less hours at your job to balance work and school.

EXERCISE 31   **Matching advice with users**

In the second column (Speaker and Listener), indicate who might be the speaker and listener for each statement. Some examples have more than one answer. Write the letters for all the possible appropriate pairs.

a. Supervisor to employee   **d.** Parent to child
b. Counselor to student   **e.** Friend to friend
c. Instructor to student

Statement	Speaker and listener
You must clean your room now.	*d*
You might think about majoring in math.	
Get a job!	
You don't have to work tonight.	
You ought to think about taking ESL.	
You must take ESL.	
You might want to consider taking ESL.	
You must take ESL before English 100.	
You may take a break now.	
You might want to study page 5 before the test.	
You should do what you want.	

More Words to Control Tone
The Power Grammar tip on page 158 gave you many words to control tone. We also use words like *perhaps*, *possibly*, and *maybe* to make our advice more acceptable to others. If we want someone to agree with us (and not say No!), we can use words like *Let's*. Be aware, however, that *let's* is better for spoken, informal language. Usually it is not used in formal writing.

▭ Writing, Editing, and Revising

EXERCISE 32 **Writing the first draft of your letter**

Write the first draft of your letter. The first paragraph will summarize Marcella's problem. The second paragraph will offer suggestions or advice. The third paragraph will be a conclusion for your letter. Although this is a letter to a fellow student, use academic or formal language. Here is the format you will use.

Leave an inch margin		Leave a half-inch margin
	Today's Date (*For example, December 9, 2005*)	
	Dear Marcella, (*Note the comma after the name*)	
	(*Indent 5 spaces here*) I understand you have a dilemma because … (*This is a suggestion for the first sentence, but you could use other openings. Just make sure you describe her problem accurately. Do this in 2–3 sentences.*)	
	(*Indent 5 spaces here*) Here are some suggestions for solving your dilemma. (*In this paragraph, you will give Marcella your best advice. Use examples to explain your suggestions. Do this in 5–7 sentences.*)	
	(*Indent 5 spaces here*) (*Write a closing sentence—like a conclusion—for your letter here.*)	
	Sincerely,	
	(*Sign your name here*)	

EXERCISE 33   Editing your letter

Check your draft letter for the correct tone. Be sure the tone is not too harsh, too strong, or unreasonable. Remember that you are offering advice to a fellow student who needs help. You cannot order her to do anything.

- Circle all the words that might help Marcella take your advice.

- Check to make sure each sentence is complete.

- Check that your letter looks like the model letter format on page 163 (e.g., make sure it has the date, a greeting, three paragraphs, and a closing).

EXERCISE 34   Doing a peer review

Exchange draft letters with a student who was not in your group for the role playing. Use Peer Review Form 4-2 in the appendix to review your classmate's draft letter. When you have made your comments, discuss them with the writer, and listen to your classmate's comments about your draft letter.

EXERCISE 35   Revising your letter

Now revise your letter. Make any changes you think will improve it. When your letter is your best work, give it to your instructor for further review.

Student Sample 10 (Nawal)

A credit card has two sides: advantages and disadvantages. In my opinion, it is more of an advantage because I can use it for many purposes. First of all, I can use it for special occasions. For example, when I go out of the country and I don't have enough money, I will use the credit card for payment. Second, I can use it to buy some things on line. In this case, I can save time. Third, I can use it to save my money because I don't have to pay cash right away. Fourth, my credit card gives me extra insurance when I rent a car. Fifth, I can build up my credit history. For example, if I don't have a good credit history, it is hard to buy something like a house. For me, a credit card is useful.

Nawal

Student Sample 11 (Tram)

Credit cards have two sides, advantages and disadvantages. For me they are very important because of the advantages. First, they are very convenient and safe. I can use them to buy some things online or when I travel. For example, when I travel, I do not want to carry much money because it's not safe. Sometimes I really want to buy something at the airport, where they do not accept payment by cash or check. So I can use a credit card. Secondly, if I pay my credit card bills on time, I can build up my credit history. That way, my good credit will allow me to buy a car or some other very expensive thing with payments over time. Last, the credit card company can provide the buyer with a guarantee. If something goes wrong with an item that I bought with my credit card, the credit card company may replace it. That's why I always pay for airplane tickets by credit card. I try to avoid the disadvantages by using credit cards carefully and controlling them.

Tram

EXERCISE 38 **Finding specific examples and details**

Reread each paragraph. Highlight specific examples and specific details.
Then put an X or check mark for each student if you can answer Yes to the
question. Discuss your answers with another student. Be sure to support
your answer with the highlighted specific examples and details. After you
have completed the chart, answer the Yes-No question that follows the chart.

Does this student have:	Waheeda	Sylvie	Nawal	Tram
Advantages of using credit cards?				
Specific examples and details explaining advantages?				
Disadvantages of using credit cards?				
Specific examples and details explaining advantages?				

Do you think that specific examples are important in writing good

paragraphs?   Yes _____   No _____

Yes, because _____

_____.

No, because _____

_____.

EXERCISE **39** **Evaluating credit cards**

Using the information these students have in their paragraphs, list the advantages and disadvantages of credit cards. Then add any other points you are aware of that are not mentioned in the students' paragraphs.

Advantages of credit cards	Disadvantages of credit cards

WEB POWER

You can find more information on how to manage credit cards wisely on the Web. Use *credit card* as your keywords and see what you can find. You can use this information in your paragraph, too.

▭ Focusing and Organizing

EXERCISE **40** **Deciding which side you will take**

Remember that your assignment is to write a paragraph in which you attempt to persuade a friend either to get a credit card or not to get a credit card. You will use the best arguments you can think of to support your advice. First, however, you must decide which side to take.

Do you think there are more advantages or disadvantages to having a credit card? Circle your answer:

> Yes (There are more advantages.)

> No (There are more disadvantages.)

Which side do you want to argue? You must choose a side, even if you believe that you could argue both for and against.

_____ I think having a credit card is necessary, and I will advise my friend to get one.

_____ I think having a credit card is a mistake, and I will advise my friend not to get one.

The Vocabulary of Taking Sides

People who are <u>in favor of</u> or <u>for</u> something are said to be <u>pro</u> (for example, *pro* capital punishment). People who are <u>against</u> something are said to be <u>not in favor of</u> or <u>anti</u> (for example, anti-abortion). The arguments for and against something are often called the ***pros**** and ***cons****. Add these terms or expressions to your Word Bank.

EXERCISE 41 Stating your point of view

Practice using the vocabulary of taking sides. State your point of view on these issues, using the term in parentheses. Use complete sentences.

1. (Example) human rights (pro)/ anti) *I am prohuman rights.*

2. capital punishment (for / against)

   _____

3. animal rights (in favor of / not in favor of)

   _____

Ask your instructor if you used the terms correctly.

EXERCISE 42 Choosing strong reasons and personal examples

Decide which reasons are the best to support your point of view about credit cards. List them in order of how strong they are. Do you have any personal examples to illustrate your major ideas?

Best reason for getting (or not getting) credit cards:

_____

_____

Example to illustrate this reason: _____

Second best reason for getting (or not getting) credit cards:

_____

_____

Example to illustrate this reason: _____

Third best reason for getting (or not getting) credit cards:

_____

_____

Example to illustrate this reason: _____

EXERCISE 43 **Thinking about your topic sentence**

You might want to use one of these models for your paragraph. Circle the words and complete the sentences to try some out.

- You should definitely (get / not get) a credit card because

    _____. (*What will be the result?*)

- (Get / Don't get) a credit card because _____

    _____. (*What can they do for/to you?*)

- I advise you to (get / avoid) credit cards because they will

    _____. (*What will happen?*)

- Have you been thinking about getting a credit card? My advice to

    you is _____.

EXERCISE 44 **Writing your topic sentence**

Write your topic sentence here:

_____

_____

_____

EXERCISE 45 **Supporting your arguments with details**

Use the strongest arguments you identified in Exercise 42. On your own paper, organize your arguments and details.

- Put your strongest argument first, then your other major points.

- For each major point, add examples and details to support it.

- Remember to link the ideas using connectors like *because* and *so* that help show the relationship between them.

EXERCISE 46 Writing your concluding sentence

Write a concluding sentence that will convince your friend to take your advice. Here are some options. Check any you might use.

_____ Repeat your main idea.

_____ Warn your friend about the consequences of not taking your advice.

_____ Remind your friend about an example you used to develop your ideas.

_____ Make a prediction about what will happen if your friend takes/doesn't take your advice.

_____ Use a proverb or a quotation that illustrates your point, for example:
"Neither a borrower nor a lender be." (William Shakespeare)
"A penny saved is a penny earned." (Benjamin Franklin)

Finding Sayings and Proverbs
You can find other sayings and proverbs in *Bartlett's Famous Quotations*. You can find this book online, too.

☐ Writing, Editing, and Revising

EXERCISE 47 Writing your first draft

You are ready to write your first draft. Remember to follow the Academic Format Standards.

EXERCISE 48 **Editing your paragraph**

Check your paragraph for errors, especially for:

_____ subject-verb agreement

_____ complete sentences

_____ parallel structure

Check the tone of your paragraph to see whether it is appropriate:

_____ Is it too strong? (Will your friend feel insulted or alarmed?)

_____ Is it too weak? (Will your friend not be persuaded or convinced by your advice?)

EXERCISE 49 **Doing a peer review**

Exchange paragraphs with a student who took the opposite point of view, if possible. In other words, if your paragraph is in favor of credit cards, give your paragraph to someone who is against credit cards. Use Peer Review Form 4-3 in the appendix to review your classmate's draft. After you have completed the form, discuss your comments with the writer and listen to her or his comments about your paragraph.

EXERCISE 50 **Revising your paragraph**

Consider your peer reviewer's comments. Then decide if you will change your paragraph. List at least two changes you may make and why:

1. _____ because

_____.

2. _____ because

_____.

3. _____ because

_____.

4. _____ because

_____.

Now revise your paragraph, if necessary.

When you are satisfied that the paragraph is your best work, give it to your instructor for further review.

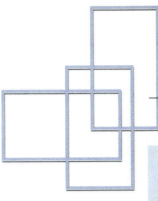

Writing Assignment 5

A *"case study"** is an assignment frequently given in college courses. Writing Assignment 5 is based on Juan's "case." First, you will learn about his financial situation. Then, after you have analyzed his case, you will give advice to Juan and his wife, Sylvia. This is a group assignment. It has many steps, which you will follow.

☐ Gathering Information

EXERCISE 51 **Discussing financial concerns**

Most students have concerns about money. With a small group of students, discuss what those concerns might be. List some of them here:

- (For example: Tuition has gone up 20 percent, and I can't afford that.)

- _____

- _____

- _____

- _____

- _____

- _____

- _____

- _____

EXERCISE 52   Looking at Juan's situation

Juan is a community college student who has almost completed his associate's degree. Because of the slowing economy, however, he may have to change his plans and not finish his degree.

To understand Juan's problem, let's look at a *timeline.** It shows major events in his life to this point.

Study the events in the timeline and the life list, and then answer the questions that follow the life list.

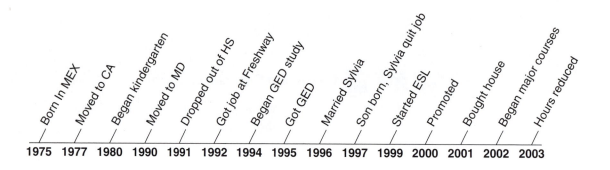

A **life list*** is another way of looking at these events:

Juan's life list

> 1975—Juan was born in Mexico.
>
> 1977—Juan and his family moved to California.
>
> 1980—Juan began kindergarten in California.
>
> 1990—Juan and his family moved to Maryland.
>
> 1991—Juan dropped out of school (before completing tenth grade).
>
> 1992—Juan got a job bagging groceries at Freshway Foodstore.
>
> 1994—Juan began studying for his GED.
>
> 1995—Juan passed the exam and received his GED.

1996—Juan married Sylvia, a nail stylist at the Nail Palace.

1997—Juan's son was born, and Sylvia quit her job to stay at home with the baby.

1999—Juan registered for ESL classes at the community college, and he prepared to work on an associate's degree in computer technology.

2000—Juan was promoted to cashier at Freshway Foodstore.

2001—Juan and Sylvia bought a house.

2002—Juan completed ESL and began classes in computer technology.

2003—Juan's job at Freshway Foodstore was reduced to part-time.

With a partner, answer these questions:

1. Do you think Juan has been successful so far with his career, family, and education?

_____

_____

2. How would you describe Juan? Use at least three terms: (for example, *hard working*)

_____

_____

_____

3. Did Juan make some good choices? What were they?

_____

_____

_____

4. Did Juan make some choices that were not very good? What were they?

_____

_____

_____

EXERCISE 53 Completing Juan's short history

Juan and his wife, Sylvia, were doing well before his work hours were reduced to part-time. For a few months, they could pay their bills by using their savings. But now they are having trouble. They consulted a financial adviser* through a community service organization to get some free advice.

The financial adviser, Mrs. Smith, asked Juan to write a short history so that she could get to know the couple better. Here is what Juan wrote.

Fill in the blanks with information from Juan's timeline and life list.

I was born in Mexico. Since I was two years old, I **have been** in the United States. First my family lived in _____. We moved to Maryland in _____. I **have lived** in Maryland ever since then. I wasn't a good student, and my family needed my help, so I dropped out of school in _____ before completing _____ grade. I know now that that was probably a mistake, but it seemed like a good idea at the time.

In _____, I got a job bagging groceries at _____. After two years of that job, I decided I needed to get my high school degree or GED because I couldn't get a promotion without it. In _____, I passed the exam and got my GED. That is the year I met Sylvia, who was a nail stylist at _____, near the store where I was working. We dated for a year, and then we got married in _____. In 1997, our son was born, and Sylvia _____ to stay home with our baby, Manuelito. We don't want to leave our child with a babysitter. What a happy time that was! But Sylvia and I decided that we had to plan for the future because we want Manuelito to go to college. We made a decision that I should try to get a degree at the _____ in computer technology because we heard there were lots of jobs in that field. I took the placement test and was disappointed to learn I would have to take ESL classes first. **I have been** in the United States as long as I can remember, but I guess I **have never learned** how to write well. I speak English great, just like anyone else, but writing **has always seemed** hard for me.

In _____, I began ESL classes, and it **has paid** off. My manager saw I was ambitious, and I **have always been** a hard worker, so he promoted me to the position of _____ at Freshway Foodstore. I was earning more money ($11 an hour) and interest rates were really low in 2001, so Sylvia and I decided to buy a _____. We found a townhouse for $120,000. It needs a lot of work, but Sylvia and I **have made** many repairs on it, and we think it is a good investment.

Everything was going really well. I completed my ESL classes in _____, and I **have taken** classes in my major, _____. But then the economy changed in 2001, especially after the terrorist attacks on the World Trade Center and the Pentagon. Although I **have worked** for Freshway Foodstore for _____ years, they had to reduce the hours of many cashiers. I was one of them. Now I am working only 20 hours per week instead of 40 hours. I **have tried** to find another job, but so far I **have had** no luck. So now Sylvia and I are trying to live on less money, and we **have spent** most of our savings. I don't want to drop out of college, as I have only four more classes to take to get my AA degree in computer technology. However, I will drop out if we can't figure a way to pay our bills. What do you think we should do?

Notice that Juan had to use verbs to connect the past to the present. The tense he often used (marked in bold in his writing) is called the present perfect. *Reread Juan's short history and notice where he uses present perfect tense. Then study the Power Grammar about using the present perfect tense in academic writing.*

POWER GRAMMAR

Using Present Perfect Tense in Academic Writing

Present perfect tense connects past time to present time. It means something like "before now."

Juan's life so far:

1. born in Mexico 1975
2. moved to Maryland 1990
3. still in Maryland

Although Juan was born in Mexico, he <u>has lived</u> in Maryland since 1990.

Because of its meaning, present perfect tense has special uses in writing. Writers often use present perfect to introduce a topic. After the introduction of the past time topic, the writer changes to use simple past tense to describe the past.

I was born in Mexico. Since I was two years old, I **have been** in the United States. First my family lived in California. We moved to Maryland in 1990.

Present perfect is also used for transitions that connect the past to the present.

I **have lived** in Maryland ever since then. I wasn't a good student, and my family needed my help, so I dropped out of school in 1991 before completing the tenth grade. I know now that that was probably a mistake, but it seemed like a good idea at the time. Sylvia and I **have made** many repairs on it. (*We still are making repairs.*)

Present perfect is made with *has* or *have* followed by the past participle of the verb.

I **have worked** for Freshway Foodstore for ten years.

The past participle for regular verbs is just the same as the past tense.

Past tense: **worked started**
Past participle: **worked started**

(Continued)

The past participle for irregular verbs usually has a different spelling and pronunciation from the simple past tense. You will find additional irregular verbs at http://esl.college. hmco.com/students.

We <u>have</u> **spent** most of our savings.
Juan <u>has</u> **been** here for many years.

(Note: _been_ and _being_ sound alike to many people but have different spellings. Be careful to write them correctly.)

EXERCISE 54 **Writing using the present perfect tense**

Use the words (and add more) to make sentences about yourself in the present perfect tense. Write at least three sentences.

1. I/live/this/city/since (year) _____. For example:

    I have lived in this city since 1979.

2. I/study/English/since (year) _____

    _____.

3. I/be/student/this college/since (year) _____

    _____.

4. _____

    _____

5. _____

    _____

W E B   P O W E R

Go to the College Writing 1 website at
http://esl.college.hmco.com/students.

EXERCISE **55** **Studying Juan and Sylvia's budget**

After Mrs. Smith, the financial adviser, read Juan's history, she asked him some questions. Here are her questions and his answers.

Add to your Word Bank any words you need to look up or ask about.

Mrs. Smith's questions	Juan's answers
1. How much is your monthly income (take-home pay) now that you are working part-time?	$800 ($880 minus taxes and health insurance premium). This is half of what I was earning before January 2003.
2. Do you have any other sources of income?	No, but we have $1,000 in savings.
3. How much per month is your mortgage payment?	$600
4. How much per month are your utilities (gas, electric, telephone)?	$125
5. How much per month is your transportation cost?	$40 (We don't have a car; we walk and take the bus.)
6. How much per month do you spend for your food and clothing?	$300
7. How much do you spend on entertainment each month? Do you make contributions to charity?	$36 for cable TV and about $60 for movies and video rental. No charitable contributions.
8. How much do you spend on college per month?	$100 per month for tuition, books, supplies.
TOTALS	Total income: $800 Total expenses: $1,261

EXERCISE 56 **Reviewing Juan and Sylvia's budget**

Look at Juan and Sylvia's budget. Answer these questions:

1. How much income do Juan and Sylvia have each month?

   _____

2. How much do Juan and Sylvia spend each month?

   _____

3. How much money do they need to cover their monthly expenses?

   _____

4. Which expenses could Juan and Sylvia reduce?

   _____

   _____

5. Make at least one suggestion for increasing their income.

   _____

   _____

   _____

☐ Focusing and Organizing

EXERCISE 57 **Understanding your writing assignment**

This is a group assignment. Here is what you will do to complete the first steps:

- In a small group, discuss your ideas about how to reduce expenses or increase income for Juan and Sylvia.
- As a group, decide on three or four ways that Juan and Sylvia could improve their financial situation.
- Make a new budget for them, showing how your suggestions could help them. In the appendix there is a Budget Worksheet you can use.

Now follow the next steps in completing this assignment.

⬜ Writing, Editing, and Revising

EXERCISE 58 Writing your paragraph

With members of your group, write a paragraph with your advice for Juan and Sylvia. Remember to develop your paragraph by following the process you have been using:

- Develop a topic sentence.
- Select and organize your major points and supporting details.
- Write an effective concluding sentence.
- Follow the Academic Format Standards.

EXERCISE 59 Editing your paragraph

With your group, edit your paragraph. Then make any necessary changes.

EXERCISE 60 Asking for a peer review

Ask other students to evaluate your paragraph and your Budget Worksheet by using Peer Review Form 4-4 in the appendix.

EXERCISE 61 Presenting your work to the class

When your group is satisfied that the paragraph is your best work, present it and the budget to the class. Use an overhead projector to present your paragraph, or make copies for the instructor and other students.

⬜ Additional Topics for More Practice and Assessment

- What is the best advice anyone has ever given you about managing responsibility? Give examples of the effect it has had on your life, especially as a student.
- What is the worst advice anyone has ever given you? Give examples of what happened when you followed that advice.
- What is your best idea about how to save time? Give examples of how it has worked for you.
- What is your best idea for saving money? Be specific. Explain how your idea could help other people.

- Describe a poor decision you made in the past about money.
- Did you ever give someone advice that he or she didn't take? Describe how you felt when the person did not do what you recommended.
- Write about a dilemma that you successfully resolved.
- Choose two decisions Juan made that you think were not wise. Explain why they were not good decisions.

⬜ Projects

- Make a timeline similar to Juan's, showing the major events of your life from birth to present time. Be sure to include jobs and education, as well as personal events.
- Make a life list of all the events you included in your timeline, using past tense verbs in your sentences (for example, *I began school in 1981*).
- Using the life list you made for yourself, combine events so that you use the present perfect tense to help explain the connection of past events and the present. Write five sentences.

Example:

Past time	Present perfect to express that you are still a student today.

I began school in 1981, and I have been a student since that time.

- Using a browser (such as Google or Yahoo), check the Internet for advice on one of these topics:
  - **a.** How to manage your finances if you lose your job
  - **b.** How to get out of debt
  - **c.** How to avoid debt
  - **d.** How to use credit cards responsibly
  - **e.** How to get financial aid for yourself

⬜ Reflection on Chapter 4

EXERCISE 62   **Writing a letter to your instructor**

Write your instructor an informal personal letter in which you talk about one of these topics:

- Which graphic organizer(s) have you found most helpful in exploring or organizing your thoughts or your writing? Which have you found to be least helpful? Why?

- Do you think your Word Bank is helping you build an academic vocabulary? What ideas do you have for making the Word Bank more useful to you?

- Did you enjoy the case study assignment in which you analyzed Juan's finances? Have you ever used the case study approach before?

- At this point in the semester, how comfortable are you with group work? Is it working for you? Why or why not?

- Be sure to use letter format and check to make sure you've edited for all the Power Grammar covered so far.

- When you have completed your letter give it to your instructor.

EXERCISE 63   **Assessing yourself**

Are you making progress in academic writing? On the next page are the writing and grammar points covered in Chapter 4. Check the box that tells how confident you feel about each.

Writing or grammar point	I feel confident about this.	I need more work on this.
Know how to use general and specific ideas in writing.		
Use graphic organizers to plan and organize writing.		
Add details by asking questions.		
Write topic sentences that fulfill a promise to the reader.		
Choose effective words to give advice or persuade people.		
Control the tone of writing through word choice.		
Look at the pros and cons of an issue.		
Know more about count and noncount nouns.		
Use present perfect verbs.		
Use a case study approach.		
Practice editing and revising.		

Before going on to Chapter 5, get more help on writing or grammar points for which you checked "I need more work on this." You can get help from:

- Your instructor
- The college writing or tutoring program
- The College Writing 1 website

WEB POWER

You will find additional exercises related to the content in this chapter at http://esl.college.hmco.com/students.

Technology and You

Academic Writing Objectives

- Use appropriate language for readers
- Know three ways to organize paragraphs
- Use apostrophes correctly
- Maintain consistent point of view
- Use correct "netiquette"

Here is what to expect in this chapter:

You will write a paragraph on	For the purpose of	Focus on these writing skills	Learn this Power Grammar	Use these graphic organizers	With this vocabulary focus
Technology and college students (choice of topics)	Description	Use three points to support topic sentence	Apostrophes for possession	Matrix to organize paragraph	
Your most useful technology	Description	Support a choice with reasons	Contractions Point of view consistency	Three-mountain plan for paragraph	Avoiding contractions in formal writing
Rules for cell phone use	Problem/solution	Take a stand and support it "Hooks"	Problem subjects: *It, There*	Matrix to analyze problem	
Netiquette—how do you measure up?	Demonstrate your e-mail netiquette	Differences between e-mail language and academic English		Matrix	E-mail language

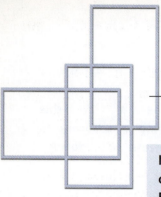

Writing Assignment 1

In the last part of the twentieth century, a technological revolution occurred, especially in the areas of information and communication. For this writing assignment, you will work with a group to produce one paragraph together about technology and college work. Before selecting the topic for your paragraph, you will think about the part technology plays in your own life.

▭ Gathering Information

EXERCISE 1 **Using technology in your life**

Some people use technology more than others. What about you? Answer these questions:

- Do you remember a time before you ever saw a television? ____ Yes ____ No

- Have you (or your family) ever owned a black-and-white television? ____ Yes ____ No

- Have you ever used a rotary dial telephone? ____ Yes ____ No

- Do you own a cellular phone? ____ Yes ____ No

- How *computer literate** are you? ____ Very ____ Somewhat ____ Not at all

- Do you use word processing? ____ All the time ____ Sometimes ____ Never

- Do you use e-mail? ____ Frequently ____ Rarely ____ Never

- Do you surf the Internet? ____ Every day ____ Sometimes

EXERCISE 2 **Discussing your answers with your group**

Discuss your answers to the questions in Exercise 1 with the group of students with whom you will be working. Then together make a list of:

- Three *problems* you and your group have because of technology

- Three *strengths* you have as students because of technology (for example, you may find research is much easier using the Internet)

- Three *things* your college should do to help you master and use technology for college success

EXERCISE 3 **Sharing ideas and choosing your topic**

Compare your list with another group's list and get new ideas. Take notes on new ideas you may want to use in your paragraph.

- Are some problems on your lists similar?   ___ Yes   ___ No

- Are some strengths on your lists similar?   ___ Yes   ___ No

- Is there some agreement on what the college   ___ Yes   ___ No
  should do to help you master technology
  for success?

Now choose your group's topic for your paragraph. Here are the choices:

- The three worst problems your group has with technology

- Three things successful college students need to know about technology

- Three ways your college could help students master technology for college success

EXERCISE **4**   **Assigning roles as team members**

Although you will develop the paragraph together, decide on some individual roles first. Write the name of each person on the lines.

- One person will be the group leader and keep the group **on task**.*

  _____

- One person will be the recorder and do the writing for the group.

  _____

- One person will be the timekeeper for the group. (Ask your instructor how much time you will have to do the parts of the assignment.) _____

EXERCISE **5**   **Writing your topic sentence**

Decide on a topic sentence that gives the readers the main idea you want to express in your paragraph. The sentence can include the three key ideas you will discuss in the paragraph, or it can make a more general statement and not specifically name the three key idea details.

Write it here:

_____

_____

_____

_____

_____

Evaluate your topic sentence:

- Does it reflect your group's opinion on your chosen topic?
- Does it state the main idea of your paragraph?
- Does it have a "hook"?

Revise your topic sentence until you can answer yes to all these questions.

EXERCISE **6**   **Writing your major points and supporting details**

Use the notes from your discussion to choose three major points that explain your topic sentence. Write the major points and the supporting details in this chart:

Topic Sentence:	
First Major Point:	Supporting Detail:
	Supporting Detail:
	Supporting Detail:
Second Major Point:	Supporting Detail:
	Supporting Detail:
	Supporting Detail:
Third Major Point:	Supporting Detail:
	Supporting Detail:
	Supporting Detail:

EXERCISE 7   Developing your conclusion

With your group, write three possible concluding sentences.

1. _____

   _____

2. _____

   _____

3. _____

   _____

Decide on the best conclusion for your paragraph, and write the sentence here:

_____

_____

EXERCISE 8   Studying the Power Grammar tip

Here is a tip to help you with your writing.

POWER GRAMMAR

Apostrophes

In written English, apostrophes are added to nouns to show possession. When you speak, the listener knows what you mean, but in writing you need to be sure your readers understand. So using apostrophes right is important in writing academic English.

| For a noun that does not end in -s, just add the apostrophe and -s. This rule applies to singular nouns and plural nouns that do not end in -s. | **Singular noun with -'s** The boy's computer Mary's cell phone A computer's drive | **Plural noun with -'s** Children's education Men's classes |

(Continued)

Most plural nouns end in -s. For these plural nouns, just add the apostrophe at the end. It looks strange, but that is the way to do it.	My classes' midterm exams The students' written English
Some names end with -s. Making these names possessive is a challenge. People do not always agree about how to make these words possessive.	Dennis' book or Dennis's book Jones' home or Jones's home
DO NOT use the apostrophe with personal pronouns (*yours, his, hers, its, ours, theirs*).	This book is **theirs**. That one is **ours**. These are **ours**. Those are **hers**. This is **yours**. **Its** technological level is high.
You probably know that apostrophes are also used for contractions. For more information on how to use them, see the website http://esl.college. hmco.com/students. But keep in mind this tip: *It's* is the contraction for *It is*. Do not confuse it with the possessive *its*.	It's my favorite software. = It is my favorite software.

EXERCISE 9 Using apostrophes correctly for possession

Ghazala's paragraph is about her experiences with the Internet. Does Ghazala need apostrophes for possession in her writing? With a partner, circle words that need them, and write the correct form above each. Remember that not every word that ends in -s needs an apostrophe.

Student Sample 1 (Ghazala)

I have some good experiences in my life with the Internet. Three months ago, I had a project to write about Afro-Americans lives. I did not know about the history of Afro-Americans. It was very hard for me to find history books at the library. I spent three days searching the librarys shelves. Then I asked my teacher. She said, "The best way is to search the Internets sources." I liked her suggestion. I searched the Internet, and I collected very good details about Afro-American peoples lives. Now I plan to use my computers resources whenever I have assignments to do.

Ghazala

EXERCISE 10 Choosing the correct spelling

Circle the right choice for each sentence.

1. This college should change it's / its rules for using the computer lab.

2. It's / Its the student's responsibility to learn word processing.

3. This computer is mine, but those computers are their's / theirs.

4. This software program belongs to the college. It's / Its their's / theirs.

5. I don't have Internet access, so I used their's / theirs.

6. It's / Its true that technology can help college students.

7. This cell phone is mine; it's / its not yours.

▭ Writing, Editing, and Revising

EXERCISE **11** Writing your first draft

As you write your first draft of your paragraph:

A. *Remember to follow the Academic Format Standards.*
B. *Make a copy of the paragraph for each member of your group so that everyone can work on it at the same time.*

EXERCISE **12** Checking your writing

Divide up the work.

- *One person should check for indentation, capitalization, and punctuation (including apostrophes).*
- *One person should check for sentence completeness.*
- *One person should check for parallel structures.*
- *One person should check for using the right tense for the right meaning.*
- *Everyone should check for spelling!*

EXERCISE **13** Reviewing group peer writing

Exchange paragraphs with another group. Review their writing while they review yours. Use the Peer Review Form for Group Paragraph 5-1 in the appendix.

Then discuss your comments with the other group. Listen to their comments on your writing.

List three things that your group will change.

1. _____

2. _____

3. _____

EXERCISE 14 Revising your paragraph

Using the other group's comments and discussion with your group, make any changes you think would improve your paragraph. You might change one or more of these:

- Your topic sentence

- Your major points

- Your supporting details

- Your concluding sentence

- Any grammar, punctuation, or spelling errors

Revise your paragraph until every member of the group is satisfied. Then turn it in. You may make more changes after your instructor has reviewed it.

EXERCISE 15 Reflecting on group writing

Freewrite for five minutes on your reactions to writing a paragraph as a group. Here are some questions to get you started writing.

- Did you enjoy working with a group on a writing assignment? Why or why not?

- Were you frustrated by the process? Why or why not?

- Do you prefer to work by yourself? Why or why not?

- Do you think the paragraph was better than one you would have written by yourself? Why or why not?

- Is writing with a group easier or more difficult than writing by yourself? Why?

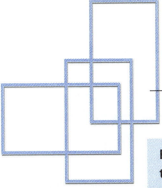

Writing Assignment 2

For this writing assignment, you will work by yourself. Choose one technological device or development that is useful to you as a college student. You will give three reasons why it is useful. You could choose:

- The cell phone
- The Internet
- E-mail
- The word processor

Gathering Information

EXERCISE 16 Deciding on your topic

You have a choice of topics. Take some time to think about which topic to choose.

- If you have a cell phone or access to the Internet, e-mail, and word processing, choose the one you think has helped you the most as a student.

- If you have used only one kind of technology, choose that.

- If you have no experience with any of the technological devices listed above:

  a. Be creative: After all, a telephone is a technological device. So are a pager, an answering machine on a telephone, a palm pilot, a television, and a VCR. Even an electric alarm clock could be a great help to a student!

  b. Ask for help: talk with your instructor to get an idea.

Once you have decided on your topic, write it here:

_____

_____

_____

EXERCISE **17**   **Listing what you know about your topic**

On a piece of paper, make a list of ways in which the device you chose has helped you as a student. You do not need to write complete sentences.

EXERCISE **18**   **Brainstorming about your topic**

Usually you brainstorm* with a group of people to solve problems. Find two or three other students who chose the same topic (the same technological device) and brainstorm for ten minutes. Similar to freewriting, brainstorming is stating every thought you have about the topic but orally with other people. Use your list from Exercise 17 to begin your brainstorming. Then try to state other reasons why your chosen technological device is great for students. Take notes on the ideas you hear that might help you write your paragraph.

▭ Focusing and Organizing

EXERCISE **19**   **Learning a new way to organize**

A new way to focus major ideas and details is the "three-mountain plan" (because your plan will resemble three mountains). Study Angel's example:

The Internet is very helpful to students.

(2)   (3)   (1)

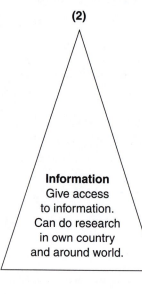
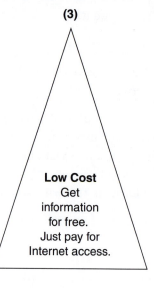

Information
Give access
to information.
Can do research
in own country
and around world.

Low Cost
Get
information
for free.
Just pay for
Internet access.

Convenience
Can read the
news, shop, be
informed about
weather, plan a trip.

EXERCISE 20 Comprehending Angel's three-mountain plan

Answer these questions:

1. Which technology did Angel choose to write on? _____
2. What three major points does he plan to use to explain why this technology is useful to students?

   _____

   _____

   _____

3. Where did he write his ideas for supporting details?

   _____

EXERCISE 21 Making a three-mountain plan

Draw a three-mountain plan for your major points and supporting details. You do not have to write entire sentences, just words that will become sentences.

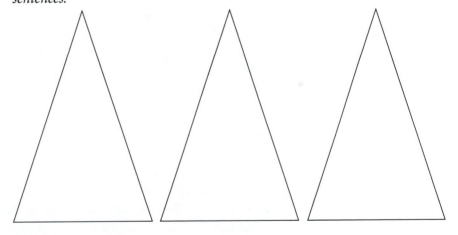

EXERCISE 22 Writing your topic sentence

Your topic sentence can be very simple. Write it here:

_____

_____

Now copy it at the top of your three-mountain plan, just as Angel did.

EXERCISE 23   **Looking at Angel's paragraphs**

Before you develop the rest of your paragraph, look at Angel's paragraphs. Study them well. Notice that he gathered so much good information that he wrote three paragraphs. He began his first paragraph with the main idea for the entire composition: The Internet is very helpful for students (it is in bold). But each paragraph has a topic sentence (underlined). Use these words. That sentence is followed by (a) supporting ideas and (b) a sentence that concludes the paragraph.

Student Sample 2 (Angel)

The Convenience of the Internet

The Internet is very helpful for students. *First of all, it is convenient.* If they have a computer with access to the Internet, they can easily read the news without the need to go out to buy the newspaper. They may also buy groceries, clothes, and books, and they receive them at home in a few days or even the same day. This is good for students who are not in their hometown or countries, have no car or other ways of transportation, or simply their campus is far away from the shopping area. In addition, they can download from the Internet programs of encyclopedias, dictionaries or translations, or thesauruses. That way, they save money buying from the stores and save time going to the libraries as well.

The Internet helps students the most when they can do research and navigate through the worldwide web. They can access any library in the country or overseas by entering the websites (www) of embassies, universities, libraries, bookstores and research companies. For example, someone from France can log on to the U.S. Library of Congress website and have access to documents, magazines, and articles. That really makes a student's life much easier since there is no barrier to get the information.

The Internet is economical. All the convenience and information of the Internet is free for most students if they use the college computer labs. If they want to have Internet access on their home computers, it is not very expensive. It is convenient for them to use the Internet whenever they want and not worry about when the college computer lab is open. In conclusion, I would suggest that every student have access to the Internet and take classes about how to use it effectively.

SPOTLIGHT ON WRITING SKILLS

What to Do When You Have More Than One Paragraph

As you gathered information for your paragraph, perhaps you, like Angel, discovered you had too much information. You may want to divide your ideas into two or three paragraphs. Remember:

- Each paragraph should have only one important or key idea.
- Each paragraph has a topic sentence with a controlling or key idea, supporting details, and a concluding sentence.

EXERCISE 24   Developing main points and supporting details

Now develop your main points and your supporting details, using your three-mountain plan. Include interesting examples from your own experience that will bring your writing to life.

EXERCISE 25   Writing your concluding sentence(s)

Your paragraph (or each of your paragraphs) should have a concluding sentence. Look at Angel's writing. What does the concluding sentence for his writing do? If you said make a recommendation, *you are correct.*

What does your *concluding sentence do?*

_____ Summarize

_____ Solve a
            problem

_____ Recommend

_____ Express a hopeful thought or
            inspirational idea

_____ Predict

Here is information on an important grammar point: consistent point of view. Study this information to use in your academic writing.

POWER GRAMMAR

Consistent Point of View

In academic writing, you must be consistent in using pronouns. This usage is called "point of view."

You can write from the "first person" point of view. (*I* is the first person singular; *we* is first person plural.)	I think cellular phones waste my time. We think the Internet opens up our world.
You can also write using the "second person" point of view. (*You* is the second person, both singular and plural.)	You should never use someone else's password. Use your own. [SINGULAR] You are members of this team. [PLURAL]
Or you can write from the "third person" point of view. (*He, she,* and *it* are third person singular; *they* is third person plural.)	A student must know the basics of computer literacy to succeed in college. He or she needs to understand word processing and Internet use. Students at some universities get free computers for their classes. They use the computers for all their work.

It is important to be consistent in using first, second, or third person pronouns. Do not shift (or change) point of view.

Some college instructors advise students not to use *you* in academic writing. Others do not like students to use *I*. Ask your instructor's advice.

EXERCISE 26 **Finding the shifts in point of view**

With a partner, circle any shifts in points of view you find in this student writing. Then, together, fix them.

> My computer is very important to me. I can do my work better because of word processing. You can check your spelling, and if there is anything wrong with the words, I can fix them. You can also get some help with grammar with your computer. Students can even get tutoring and help on papers they are writing. So they get better grades and then they are happy. So be sure to learn to use a computer!

EXERCISE 27 **Looking at Angel's point of view**

Look at Angel's paragraphs on page 202. Circle all the personal pronouns he uses.

- Which person does Angel use?
- Is he consistent throughout his paragraph?

EXERCISE 28 **Looking at Kwaku's point of view**

Circle the personal pronouns in Kwaku's paragraph below.

- Which person does Kwaku use?
- Is he consistent throughout his paragraph?
- Why does he use *he* and *him* several times?

Student Sample 3 (Kwaku)

> The Internet has been very helpful to me. As a matter of fact, it has made me successful in everything I planned to do this year. Last midterm, I was given a big assignment to do by my biology teacher on the research of how plants develop their green leaves. It was really a big research project for me to do. I went home and explained it to my dad and asked if he can help me with this research since he is more interested in plant growth. He didn't have any idea about this research, so it was up to me to find it on my own. I went to the Internet and browsed to the Department of Agriculture's Web page. Lucky for me, I found my research on that site and even learned more about how plants help us. The Internet has helped me a lot.

Kwaku

▭ Writing, Editing, and Revising

EXERCISE 29 Writing your paragraph(s)

Write the first draft of your paragraph or paragraphs on the technology that has helped you most as a student.

EXERCISE 30 Checking your writing for person consistency

Which person did you write in? Did you change point of view? If so, correct the personal pronouns so that the paragraph has just one voice. Then check which person you used.

_____ First person (*I, me, my, mine*; or *we, us, our, ours*)

_____ Second person (*you, your, yours*)

_____ Third person (*he/she/it, him, his*; or *they, them, their, theirs*)

EXERCISE 31 Checking your writing for other problems

Now take some time to edit your writing.

- Did you use the Academic Format Standards?
- Did you check all sentences to be sure they are complete?
- Does each paragraph have a topic sentence?
- Does each paragraph have a concluding sentence?
- Did you use the correct verb tenses for the correct meaning?
- Did you check for correct use of apostrophes?
- Is this the best work you can do?

EXERCISE 32 Doing a peer review

Exchange papers with a classmate. Use Peer Review Form 5-2 in the appendix to check each other's papers on important points. Then discuss your comments with your partner.

EXERCISE 33 Revise your writing

Make any changes to the content and organization of your writing that you think will improve it. Then give it to your instructor.

SPOTLIGHT ON WRITING SKILLS

Avoid Contractions in Written English

You know that spoken and written English are different. For example, in formal written English, contractions are not used. Read the Power Grammar tip to find out more.

POWER GRAMMAR

Contractions

Contractions are a basic feature of spoken English and informal writing, but in academic written English, you should not use contractions. Instead, you should write out both words.

Contractions occur when two words are **combined**, and some sounds are left out or changed. An apostrophe shows where a letter was left out.

*Spoken Version**	Written Version
He doesn't	He does not
We aren't	We are not
They don't	They do not
I'm	I am
That's	That is
I've	I have
She isn't	She is not
You haven't	You have not
I'll	I will

Using contractions is natural when we speak. We leave out or change some sounds, making our speech smoother.

It's is the contraction for *It is*. Do not confuse it with the possessive **its**.

It's my favorite software. | It is my favorite software.

Some contractions are not regular in how they are formed. They look very different from the full version.

I won't = I will not
You can't = you cannot

The contraction -'s can be used for two verbs. It is pronounced the same way in both uses, but the meaning depends on the *context*,* the words that surround the verb.

He's . . .   's = has   's = is

He's been here before. | He's a student in my college.

(Continued)

You can use the contraction with these pronouns: *He's, she's, it's*	She has been here before.	<u>She's</u> a good friend. He is a student in my college. She is a good friend.
The contraction -*'d* can be used for two verbs. It is pronounced the same way in both uses.	She'd . . .	**'d** = had	**'d** = would
You can use it with all the pronouns except *it*: *I'd, you'd, he'd, she'd, we'd, they'd*		She'd studied computers in high school. She had studied computers in high school.	She'd like to study computers in college, too. She would like to study computers in college, too.
	They'd	They'd already sent their e-mail.	They'd like to log off now.
In formal or academic writing, the full form is usually used, except when you are quoting someone's speech. In this case, be careful to put the apostrophe in the correct place.	I would like to go to the lab. My friend said to me, "**I'd** like to go to the lab."	

EXERCISE 34 Writing out the contractions correctly

Write the correct written version of the underlined contraction in each sentence. The first one has been completed for you.

1. Computers <u>aren't</u> as expensive now as they were last year.   *are not*

2. <u>He'd</u> like to learn programming when he completes his ESL courses.   _____

3. <u>It's</u> been three years since Alicia began Information Technology classes.   _____

4. <u>She's</u> studied networking since summer semester.   _____

5. <u>He's</u> very confused about how to use call waiting on his telephone.   _____

6. The students <u>can't</u> tell the difference between IST and IT classes.   _____

7. <u>We'd</u> like to take a break before continuing the class.   _____

8. You <u>aren't</u> familiar with software, but <u>you'll</u> learn.   _____

9. <u>There's</u> a big difference between PCs and Macs.   _____

10. <u>You're</u> right about laser printers.   _____

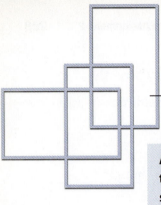

Writing Assignment 3

Although cellular phones are very useful, sometimes people who use them seem rude or impolite to others. Many people think there should be rules for using cell phones. Write a paragraph that suggests rules for polite cell phone use.

List two to four rules for polite cell phone use. For each rule, explain why the rule is needed and give an example to show the problem. Conclude your paragraph by telling how the rules would solve the problems.

Remember: You will probably not use all of the information you gather. You may even have enough information for two paragraphs!

Gathering Information

EXERCISE 35 Thinking about your cell phone experiences

Take five minutes to either draw a mind map or freewrite about experiences you have had in which people (maybe yourself) have annoyed others because of how they used their cell phones.

EXERCISE 36 Discussing with your classmates

In a small group or with the whole class, discuss the writing assignment and your ideas. Get the ideas of your classmates about this topic, especially:

- situations or places where cell phones are used

- problems cell phones cause in each situation

- solutions or rules that would help

Add to the ideas in the matrix below about cell phone use:

Situation	Problem	Solution or rule
In the classroom		
In the library	*Example: It interrupts your concentration*	
In hospitals		
In public transportation		
In cars		*Example: A law forbidding cell phone use by drivers.*

EXERCISE **37**   **Deciding on how to focus your ideas and details**

Use one of the following techniques to focus your ideas and details:

- An outline
- A matrix or table
- The three-mountain plan

Circle the one you will use. Why did you choose it?

_____

_____

SPOTLIGHT ON WRITING SKILLS

Hooking the Audience

Whenever you write academic prose, you write for one or more readers. You want your readers (for this assignment, your classmates and your instructor) to agree with you about cell phone rules. So begin your paragraph with a hook to get them interested in reading your ideas. Remember, a hook is usually the first sentence in a paragraph. It can be the topic sentence of the paragraph, or the topic sentence can be the second sentence.

EXERCISE 38 Finding a hook

Read each of these paragraph beginnings. Then ask yourself if the sentence has a good hook. Would you want to keep reading?

1. I totaled my car because of a cell phone.   ____ Yes   ____ No

2. As we all know, cell phones have just been invented within the past decade, but many people misuse them very badly in different ways.   ____ Yes   ____ No

3. It is necessary to have rules about cell phones.   ____ Yes   ____ No

4. The cell phone has caused me a lot of trouble in my life.   ____ Yes   ____ No

5. I think there should be rules of etiquette for using cell phones.   ____ Yes   ____ No

Which of these hooks do you like best? Why?

_____

_____

_____

_____

▭ Focusing and Organizing

EXERCISE 39 **Writing your topic sentence**

Write a topic sentence with a hook here:

_____

_____

_____

_____

_____

Ask another student if the topic sentence has a good hook and circle the answer and explain why.

    Yes   *No*

Why? _____

_____

_____

Keep working on your topic sentence until the answer is Yes.

EXERCISE 40 **Learning about problem subjects**

Two little words that cause many students trouble when they write are there *and* it. *Study the Power Grammar tip to clear up any confusion you may have about these words.*

POWER GRAMMAR

Problem Subjects

You know that every sentence (or clause) must have a subject and a verb. Some subjects in English cause trouble for learners.

When the sentence begins with *there*, the verb has to agree with the noun that follows *there* in the sentence.	There **is** a **cell phone** in my book bag. There **are** two **cell phones** in my book bag.
When people speak, they sometimes use *there is* or *there's* with a plural noun. This is not considered correct in academic writing.	~~There's some computers on the table.~~ No There are some computers on the table. Yes
Sometimes *it* is the subject. Do not leave it out even if it does not seem important to you.	**It** is a fast-working virus. **It** is true that computers can crash. **It's** a hacker who introduced the virus into the system. [For spoken English]
Many languages leave out the subject if it is obvious who or what is meant. You cannot do this in English. There must be a subject.	~~Is a new terminal.~~ No It is a new terminal. Yes ~~Is advanced technology.~~ No It is advanced technology. Yes

EXERCISE 41   **Making sentences with there**

Make a sentence with each group of words. Do not change the order of the words, but add any necessary words and change the word forms if necessary. Use correct capitalization and punctuation.

1. there/a/CD burner/my computer

_____

_____

2. there/three/passwords/my computer

_____

_____

3. there/seven/speed dial numbers/Ali's cell phone

_____

_____

4. there/too many/technological devices/difficult/understand

_____

_____

5. there/advantages/disadvantages/PC /Macs

_____

_____

EXERCISE **42** **Making sentences with it**

Work with a partner. Write sentences about technology, beginning each sentence with It. _Use each of the words in your sentence, changing them as necessary. Add any other words to make your sentence powerful. Remember to use the correct verb tense for each sentence. (Hint: Look for the words that tell you whether the correct tense is past, present, or future.)_

1. Cell phone/car/yesterday (_for example, note that "yesterday" signals past tense_) It was lucky I had my cell phone yesterday when my

broke down.

2. Rude/cell phone/in class

_____

3. Better/headset/cell phone/car

_____

4. Expensive/call out of state/last night

_____

5. Difficult/select/telephones/many choices

_____

EXERCISE 43 **Checking for completeness**

Look at every supporting sentence you wrote in your paragraph about cell phones. Underline each subject and verb in each clause. Remember to:

- *be careful with* there *and* it *as subjects.*
- *avoid contractions.*
- *use apostrophes correctly in possessives.*

W E B P O W E R

You will find additional exercises related to the content in this chapter at the College Writing 1 website
http://esl.college.hmco.com/students.

EXERCISE 44 **Writing your concluding sentence**

Just as you tried to find a good hook for your first sentence, try to end your paragraph with a concluding sentence the reader will remember. Write your concluding sentence here:

_____

_____

_____

Now ask a partner to read it and evaluate it. Your partner should check one item for your conclusion:

_____ This concluding sentence is fascinating, and I will never forget it.

_____ This concluding sentence is all right, but by tomorrow I will have forgotten it.

_____ This concluding sentence put me to sleep zzzzzzzzzzzzzz.

What is one thing your partner suggests that you could do to improve your concluding sentence?

_____

_____

Revise your concluding sentence if your partner did not check the first box.

EXERCISE 45 Editing your writing

Check your writing for:

- Academic Format Standards
- Correct punctuation
- Proper use of apostrophes
- One problem you have had in past paragraphs. Write what that problem is:

_____

_____

EXERCISE 46 Doing a group peer review

With two or three other classmates, exchange paragraphs. Each student should try to read three paragraphs.

After your group has finished reading the paragraphs, discuss which was the most persuasive. Why was it the most persuasive?

- Was the hook particularly interesting?
- Were the examples especially detailed and realistic?
- Was the concluding sentence strong and convincing?

The writer of the most persuasive paragraph in each group will read that paragraph to the class.

EXERCISE 47 Revising your paragraph

From what you learned by reading and listening to other students' paragraphs, you can revise your own paragraph. List three things you will do to revise your paragraph:

1. _____

_____

2. _____

_____

3. _____

_____

Then give it to your instructor.

EXERCISE 48 **Practicing with more examples**

Two students in the same class were writing paragraphs on cell phone rules when another student's cell phone rang. These students both included the incident as an example of the problems cell phones cause in the classroom. Read both examples (underlined). Then decide which student used the incident more effectively in her or his writing. Discuss your answer with other students in your class.

Student Sample 4 (Ahmad)

For example, if we put a sign saying "No Cell Phones," it would be better. When Mostafa's cell phone rang, we were listening to the teacher. As I wrote, it is not necessary to have a law for cell phones. <u>When I was thinking about it, Mariala's cell phone rang.</u> I turned off my cell phone when I came into class.

Student Sample 5 (Sohelee)

In the classroom, the students need to turn off their cell phones because it bothers other students. For example, almost every one of my classmates has a cell phone, but they never turn them off. Every single day, I see when their cell phone rings, they run outside the room and start to talk. <u>Oh, no! Right now Mariala's cell phone is ringing. She is leaving the room, but her phone call has interrupted all the students.</u> We really need a rule that there will be no cell phones inside the classroom.

SPOTLIGHT ON WRITING SKILLS

Choose Language Appropriate for Your Reader

Whether you are writing an e-mail to a friend, a thank-you note to your grandmother, a memo to your work supervisor, or a note to your teacher, you should consider how your choice of language will affect your reader. For example, if you began your note to your grandmother, "Hey, Dude!" your grandmother probably would not appreciate it. So, beginning with words, and then with sentences, you should think about your reader as you write. Do not be too casual or conversational if you are writing to your instructor, your supervisor, or someone else in a position of authority. Use formal language when you are not sure how informal to be.

EXERCISE 49   Grading e-mails for appropriateness

Here are some e-mail messages from students to their instructors.

With a partner, evaluate each one and give each a grade of A, B, C, D, or F. Write your comments in the box at the right.

1

Comment Box

Good morning, Ms. Allie Smith this is student An Kim. I am sorry that I couldn't call you yesterday, but I was feeling sick. I had a stomach virus. Today I feel better. I already have yesterday's homework. I just wanted you to know. Thanks!

1
A B C D F
Comments:

2

Hi m's smith how are you? Would you please tell me what gread i got.

2
A B C D F
Comments:

3

Can idrop my research paper again in your mail box between 9–9:30 am tomorrow?? Can icome and pick it up in your mail box this Monday morning?

3
A B C D F
Comments:

4

Thank you, Mrs. Smith, I got your e-mail.

4
A B C D F
Comments:

5 Comment Box

Hello, and happy new year. I always like everyone congratulate me when I am happy or at least there is one reason for being happy. Now, it is the best time for sharing our happiness although Iranian's new year begins at the first day of spring and normally we don't celebrate this new year as you do. However, I am just sending you this e-mail from all my heart for saying:

"Have a wonderful time!"

Best wishes,

Amina B_____

5
A B C D F
Comments:

6

Whassup teacher? I wanna know b4 tusday what I missed cuz I was real busy 4 three wks so I coulnt go to class. Firstable I got this ticket cuz me n my cussin was speeding in my car n we hadda go to cort and then they took away my drivers liscensce so I now I gotta get a ride from my sister. Maybe I can get t o class next week. Hope I didn't miss anything.

6
A B C D F
Comments:

Share your grades with your classmates. If you disagree, discuss until you reach an agreement about the grades.

With your partner, rewrite one of the messages so that it is appropriate.

Writing Assignment 4

Most students use e-mail often to stay in touch with friends, family, and instructors. E-mail is so new that sometimes users offend others without realizing it. **Etiquette*** means the forms and rules of proper behavior required by custom among people—in other words, polite behavior. What do you think "netiquette" means?

This is a very short writing assignment. First, complete Exercises 50, 51, 52, and 53 to review good e-mail practices. Then, send your instructor an e-mail message that shows you understand good e-mail netiquette and the appropriate language for her or him.

Your e-mail message should do the following:

- Briefly explain to your instructor one new thing you learned about netiquette.
- Show that you know how to choose appropriate language for your audience (your instructor).

⬚ Gathering Information

EXERCISE 50 Testing your netiquette

Circle T (True) if the statement describes you or F (False) if it does not.

T   F   **1.** I love to forward jokes to everyone on my mailing list.

T   F   **2.** I like to use e-mail to write to my instructor because I don't have to worry about spelling, punctuation, and grammar.

T   F   **3.** At work, I can say whatever I like about my boss in e-mail messages because he won't see it, as I have a password.

T   F   **4.** When I delete a message, it's gone.

T   F   **5.** I write long e-mail messages to impress my boss.

T   F   **6.** I write everything in CAPITAL LETTERS and don't have to worry about capitalization.

T   F   **7.** I like e-mail because I can send long files as attachments.

T   F   **8.** I forward all virus warnings to all my friends.

T   F   **9.** I give my password to my best friends so that they can use my e-mail.

T   F   **10.** I use the cute instant messaging shortcuts in my college assignment writing, too: For example: LOL ☺ (laugh out loud), B4 (before), w/o (without), b/c (because), XOXO (hugs and kisses), sry (sorry), ROTFL (rolling on the floor laughing), nmjcu (not much just chillin', you?).

EXERCISE 51 **Discussing your answers with your class**

In a small group, discuss your answers. What did you notice about your

answers? _____

_____

_____

Look at the bottom of the page for the answer.

Give yourself a score. Count the number of times you answered False. Circle your score. Then, do Exercise 52 to analyze the reasons for the answers.

10	False = 100%	Congratulations! You really know how to use e-mail correctly.
8–9	False = 80%–90%	Excellent!
7–8	False = 70%–80%	Very good! Brush up on the points you missed.
5–6	False = 50%–60%	Okay, but you need to learn more about e-mail.
0–4	False = 0%–40%	Do not use e-mail again until you finish the next exercise!

For good netiquette, you should answer F for all questions.

EXERCISE 52 Explaining reasons why

With other students, complete this chart to explain why each answer in the quiz is False. If you have an example, add it.

Statement	This is bad netiquette because ...	Examples to illustrate?
1. I love to forward jokes to everyone on my mailing list.		
2. I like to use e-mail to write to my instructor because I don't have to worry about spelling, punctuation, and grammar.		
3. At work, I can say whatever I like about my boss in e-mail messages because he won't see it, as I have a password.		
4. When I delete a message, it's gone.		
5. I write long e-mail messages to impress my boss.		
6. I write everything in CAPITAL LETTERS and don't have to worry about capitalization.		
7. I like e-mail because I can send long files as attachments.		
8. I forward all virus warnings to all my friends.		
9. I give my password to my best friends so that they can use my e-mail.		
10. I use the cute instant messaging shortcuts in my college assignment writing, too: for example: LOL (laugh out loud), B4 (before), w/o (without), b/c (because), XOXO (hugs and kisses), sry (sorry), ROTFL (rolling on the floor laughing), nmjcu (not much just chillin', you?).		

EXERCISE **53** **Learning more netiquette**

Answer these questions.

1. Is it necessary to tell the instructor your ___ Yes ___ No
   name when you e-mail?
2. Do you need to have a salutation ___ Yes ___ No
   (Dear _____,) when you e-mail?
3. Do you need a closing (Sincerely,) ___ Yes ___ No
   when you e-mail?

WEB POWER

More Information on Netiquette

Using *netiquette* as the keyword, find more ideas on the
Web for polite use of the Internet.

▭ Focusing and Organizing

Review the information you learned from the exercises in the last
several pages. Select one new piece of information about netiquette that
you have learned to write about to your instructor.

▭ Writing, Editing, and Revising

EXERCISE **54** **Writing your e-mail message**

Write on paper a draft of your e-mail message intended for your instructor.

EXERCISE **55** **Doing a peer review**

*Exchange your message with a partner. As you read your partner's e-mail,
mark any language errors. If you think your partner has been too informal
with language, give specific examples from the e-mail to your partner.*

Revise your e-mail, using your partner's comments as a guide.

Send your e-mail to your instructor.

☐ Additional Topics for More Practice and Assessment

- Some people believe that letter writing is becoming a lost art, as people use e-mail and telephones to communicate with each other. Do you agree? Explain why or why not.
- Some states have laws that make the use of cell phones while driving illegal. Write a paragraph explaining why such laws are good or bad and why.
- What is the law in your state on the use of cell phones while driving? Use the Internet to find out, if you do not know.
- If you have a PDA (personal digital assistant), write a paragraph explaining to your class how it has helped you be organized (if it has). If it has not helped you, explain why students should not waste their money on this technological device.
- If you were to be stranded on a desert island by yourself and could take with you one technological device, what would it be and why? Give three reasons for your choice.

☐ Projects

- Does your college have published rules for the use of cell phones? If not, develop rules for your college. You could submit them to the student government, the school newspaper, or simply give them to your instructor. Remember to use appropriate language for the audience.
- Some people believe that using cell phones damages your health. Go online and learn more about this. Search for information, using keywords like *cell phone dangers* or *cell phone health risks*. Then present your information to your class.
- Use a Venn diagram to compare two technological devices. Then write a paragraph based on the diagram.
- Many people have difficulty learning to use technology because they do not understand the ***jargon*,*** or specialized language of a trade, profession, or group, used in the directions. Write instructions to teach someone to do one thing, using language that anyone could understand. Then teach someone that skill. For example:

Program a VCR to record a television program
Copy a word processing file from one drive to another
Use a computer's spell checker or grammar checker
Make a simple PowerPoint presentation
Retrieve messages from a phone

▭ Reflection on Chapter 5

EXERCISE 56 **Reviewing what you have learned**

Here are some of the objectives for Chapter 5. Check the ones you feel confident about:

_____ Use appropriate language for readers

_____ Know three ways to organize paragraphs

_____ Use apostrophes correctly

_____ Maintain consistent point of view

_____ Use correct netiquette

If you do not feel confident about one or more of these objectives, list two steps you could take to learn more:

_____

_____

_____

EXERCISE 57 **Moving on**

Congratulations! You have completed Book 1. This book was designed to help you with all steps of the writing process, from *developing your ideas,* to *focusing and organizing* them, to *writing them with clarity and correctness.*

Write an e-mail to the author and the publisher, telling whether you feel you have achieved these goals or have made progress toward them. Send an e-mail to college_esl@hmco.com.

Good luck as you continue on your way to excellent academic writing and success.

WEB POWER

You will find additional exercises related to the content in this chapter at http://esl.college.hmco.com/students.

Appendix 1

Chapter 1 Word Bank

Directions: Some words are very important for college work. They are identified in each chapter by an asterisk (*).

Use this Word Bank to "deposit" the word or term in your "account." It will pay great dividends! The first word has been "deposited" for you. Complete the others marked by the * in the chapter. Add any other words or terms you wish to learn that are not marked with an asterisk in the text.

Word or term	Sentence or phrase and page	Meaning	My mastery level of the word or term		
			I understand its meaning.	I can use it in a sentence.	I can spell it correctly.
edit					
peers					
Venn diagram					
brackets					
curly brackets					
closing					

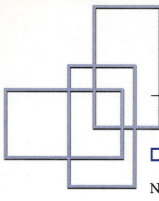

Appendix 2

CHAPTER 2

▭ Paragraph Checklist 2-1

Name of Writer: _____

Name of Peer Reviewer: _____

Question	Yes	No	Can't tell
1. Is there a topic sentence that has the main idea(s)?			
2. Are there enough details or examples to explain the keywords in the topic sentence?			
3. Does the concluding sentence have an interesting idea?			
4. Do the verbs agree with the subjects?			
Write one specific thing that you agreed or disagreed with in the paragraph:			

⬜ Study Strategy Plan 2-2

Name:

My major learning strength(s)

- ▪
- ▪

Study strategies I already use:

Study strategies I would like to try:

☐ Peer Review Form 2-3

Name of Writer: _____

Name of Peer Reviewer: _____

Question	Yes	No	Can't tell
1. Can you tell from the first sentence which topic the writer chose?			
2. Is there a topic sentencethat has the main idea(s)?			
3. Are there enough details or examples to explain the keywords in the topic sentence?			
4. Does the concluding sentence have an interesting idea?			
5. Do the verbs agree with the subjects?			

Write here any sentences with subject-verb agreement problems:

Question	Yes	No	Can't tell
6. Is the correct tense used for each verb?			

Write here any sentences with problems with tense:

7. Write one specific thing you liked or disliked in the paragraph:

▭ Chapter 2 Word Bank

Word or term	Sentence or phrase and page	Meaning	My mastery level of the word or term		
			I understand its meaning.	I can use it in a sentence.	I can spell it correctly.
tactile	A student who is a tactile learner usually likes to use her or his sense of touch. (p. 48)	Capable of being felt by the sense of touch			
visually					
kinesthetic					
symbol					
freewriting					
keywords					
supporting sentences					
format					
draft	Write the first draft of your paragraph. (p. 59)	A piece of writing that is not yet in its finished form. Sometimes called a "rough draft."			
revise					

▭ Perceptual Learning Preferences Survey

By Kate Kinsella (1993)

DIRECTIONS: *This survey has been designed to help you and your teachers better understand the ways you prefer to learn. Think about your most recent school experiences while you read each of the following statements. Then place an X on the response line that most accurately describes how you learn.*

		Usually	Sometimes	Rarely
1.	I can remember most of the information I have heard in a lecture or class discussion without taking notes.			
2.	I learn more by reading about a topic than by listening to a lecture or a class discussion.			
3.	I learn more about a subject when I can use my hands to make or draw something.			
4.	When I study new material, I learn more easily by looking over visual aids in a chapter, such as charts and illustrations, rather than by reading the assigned pages.			
5.	Talking about a subject with someone else helps me better understand my own ideas.			
6.	I take notes during class lectures and discussions and read them carefully several times before a test.			
7.	When I read a textbook, newspaper, or novel, I picture the ideas or story in my mind.			
8.	I am skilled with my hands and can easily repair things or put things together.			
9.	I remember information that I have discussed in class with a partner or a small group better than information that I have read or written about.			

		Usually	Sometimes	Rarely
10.	I get confused when I try to figure out graphs and charts that do not come with a written explanation.			
11.	When I read, I underline or highlight ideas to make the main ideas stand out and to not get distracted.			
12.	I remember information well by listening to tapes.			
13.	I am physically coordinated and do well at sports.			
14.	To remember a new word, I must hear it and say it.			
15.	I would rather see a film on a subject than listen to a lecture or read a book or magazine article.			
16.	I prefer reading a newspaper or magazine as a source of news rather than listening to the radio or watching the television.			
17.	I make drawings in my study notes or on study cards to remember new vocabulary and important material.			
18.	I read assigned material and notes aloud to myself to concentrate and understand better.			
19.	When I listen to an explanation or lecture, I form mental images or pictures to understand better.			
20.	When I am not sure how to spell a word, I write it different ways to see what looks most correct.			
21.	I best understand homework or test instructions by reading them on the board or on a handout rather than by just listening to them.			
22.	It is easier for me to remember illustrations and charts in textbooks if they are done in bright colors.			

		Usually	Sometimes	Rarely
23.	I prefer to watch the television or listen to the radio for news rather than to read a newspaper or a magazine.			
24.	I understand and remember more about a subject from a field trip than from a lecture or a textbook.			
25.	To remember a new word, I must see it several times.			
26.	Before making or drawing something, I first picture in my mind what my completed project will look like.			
27.	I find it difficult to figure out what to do on homework assignments when the teacher just gives us a handout without discussing it in class.			
28.	I write or draw while listening to a lecture or a class discussion in order to concentrate and not get restless.			
29.	I have difficulty understanding a new term if I have only a definition with no examples or illustrations.			
30.	I regularly read newspapers, magazines, or books for pleasure and information.			
31.	When I am learning about a new subject, I get more interested and remember much more if I can have "hands-on" experience such as drawing, building a model, or doing a lab experiment.			
32.	When I have homework reading assignments, I take notes or summarize the main ideas in writing.			

☐ Perceptual Learning Preferences Survey: Scoring Guide

DIRECTIONS: *Each of the checks you entered on the survey has a point value:*

USUALLY = 3 points; SOMETIMES = 2 points; RARELY = 1 point.

For each column, find the item number on the survey and enter the point value on the line to the right. Then add the total number of points in each column.

Visual/ Verbal		Visual/ Nonverbal		Auditory		Visual/Tactile Kinesthetic	
Number	Points	Number	Points	Number	Points	Number	Points
2.		4.		1.		3.	
6.		7.		5.		8.	
10.		14.		9.		11.	
16.		17.		12.		13.	
21.		19.		15.		20.	
25.		22.		18.		24.	
30.		26.		23.		28.	
32.		29.		27.		31.	
Total:	Total:	Total:	Total:	Total:	Total:	Total:	Total:

In the space below, list your perceptual learning preferences, from your highest score to your lowest score. Your highest total indicates your perceptual learning preference(s). Your next highest total indicates another strong preference, especially if the two numbers are close.

Perceptual Learning Preferences

1. _____

2. _____

3. _____

4. _____

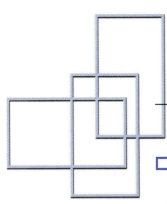

Appendix 3

🞏 Goal Planning Step-by-Step Form

My specific goal:		
Step 1		Complete by:
Step 2		Complete by:
Step 3		Complete by:
Step 4		Complete by:
Step 5		Complete by:
Step 6		Complete by:

▭ Peer Review Form 3-1

Specific Goal Plan Paragraph

Name of Writer: _____

Name of Peer Reviewer: _____

Date: _____

Organization	Yes	No
Is there a topic sentence?		
Is the topic sentence a complete sentence with a subject and a verb?		
Are the steps in a logical order?		
Are there enough details to understand how the goal will be achieved?		
Are the connectors between ideas helpful to the reader?		
Is there a conclusion?		
Is there a "hook" to interest the reader?		
Content		
What is one thing you really liked about the paragraph? (Be specific.)		
What is one suggestion you would like to make to the writer? (Be specific.)		

Format	Yes	No
Does the paragraph follow the academic format standards?		
Typed or neatly handwritten on one side of the paper		
Used 8½" by 11" paper		
Name, class, date, and other required information in proper place		
Holes on left side of loose-leaf paper		
1" margin on left, ½" margin on right		
Only first sentence indented		

▭ Peer Review Form 3-2

The Real Me Paragraph

Name of Writer: _____

Name of Peer Reviewer: _____

Date: _____

Organization	Yes	No
Is there a topic sentence?		
Is the topic sentence a complete sentence with a subject and a verb?		
Are the steps in a logical order?		
Are there enough major details to understand the writer's personality?		
Are there enough minor details to explain the major details?		
Are the connectors between ideas helpful to the reader?		
Is there a conclusion?		

Content

What questions would you like the writer to answer with details to put in the paragraph?

What is one thing you really liked about the paragraph? (Be specific.)

What is one suggestion for the writer? (Be specific.)

▭ Read-Around Peer Review Form 3-3

Decision-Making Process

Writer's Name: _____

Date: _____

Peer reviewer's initials	Criteria	Yes	No	Can't tell/ don't know
	1. Is there a clear topic sentence?			
	2. Are there at least two <u>major</u> details?			
	3. Are there enough <u>minor</u> details to explain the major details?			
	4. Is the organization of major and minor details clear and easy to follow?			
	5. Are the ideas connected logically through words that help the reader understand?			
	6. Is there an effective conclusion?			
	7. Did the writer follow the Academic Format Standards? (Note any problems in the "Can't tell/don't know" column.)			
	8. Are the decision matrices attached to the draft?			
	9. What did you like most about this paragraph?			
	10. Suggest one way this paragraph could be improved:			

☐ Chapter 3 Word Bank

Word or term	Sentence or phrase and page	Meaning	My mastery level of the word or term		
			I understand its meaning.	I can use it in a sentence.	I can spell it correctly.
hook					
linking words					
ordinal numbers					
infinitives					
boldface					
5 Ws and 1H questions					
unique					
criterion, criteria					
matrix, matrices					

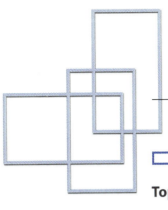

Appendix 4

☐ Peer Review Form 4-1

Topic: Managing Time to Meet Responsibilities

Writer's Name: _____

Peer Reviewer's Name: _____

Question	Yes	No
1. Is the topic sentence a clear "promise" for the paragraph?		
2. Are there major points to support the topic sentence?		
3. Are there interesting examples to illustrate major points?		
4. Are there enough details so that you get a full picture of the writer's responsibilities?		
5. Does the concluding sentence leave you with something interesting to remember or think about?		
6. What did you like best about this paragraph?		
7. Give one suggestion for improving the paragraph:		

▭ Peer Review Form 4-2

Topic: Giving Advice to Marcella in a Letter

Writer's Name: _____

Peer Reviewer's Name: _____

Question	Yes	No
1. Is the letter format correct and complete?		
2. Does the first paragraph accurately describe Marcella's dilemma?		
3. Is the advice in the second paragraph clear and easy to understand?		
4. Is the advice useful?		
5. Is the tone of the language right (not too strong or weak)?		
What do you like best about this letter?		
Do you have any suggestions for the writer?		

Peer Review Form 4-3

Topic: Arguing For or Against Credit Cards

Name: _____

Question	Yes	No (if no, explain)	Not sure
1. Does the topic sentence clearly state whether the writer is for or against credit cards?			
2. Are there two or three reasons for being for or against credit cards?			
3. Are there examples to support the writer's argument?			
4. Is the concluding sentence effective?			
5. Do you think the paragraph is a convincing argument either for or against credit cards?			
6. Is the tone of the paragraph right for a friend?			
7. Did the writer change your mind about credit cards?			

What is the best thing about this paragraph?

How could the writer improve this paragraph?

☐ Peer Review Form 4-4

Topic: Giving Financial Advice to Juan and Sylvia

Names of Group Members: _____

Names of Peer Reviewers: _____

Question	Yes	Partly	No
1. Does the paragraph have a main idea?			
2. Does the paragraph have three or four specific pieces of advice?			
3. Does the advice seem sensible and logical?			
4. Does the tone of the advice seem right for Juan and Sylvia?			
5. If Juan and Sylvia take the advice, will their financial situation improve?			
6. Is the Budget Worksheet attached?			
7. Does the budget correctly reflect the savings or increased income resulting from the advice? (Do the figures add up?)			
8. If you were Juan and Sylvia, would you use the suggestions of this group?			
9. What did you like best about this group's paragraph?			
10. Give one suggestion to improve the paragraph and budget:			

☐ **Budget Worksheet for Chapter 4 Writing Assignment**

Topic: Giving Financial Advice to Juan and Sylvia

Names of Group Members: _____

Group Name: _____

Suggestions for spending less	Current monthly expenses	Monthly savings if recommendation is followed	Monthly savings
		Total Monthly Savings	
Suggestions for earning more	**Current monthly income**	**Monthly income if recommendation is followed**	**Increase in monthly income**
		Total Increase in Monthly Income	
		GRAND TOTAL INCREASE (Total Savings + Total Increase in Monthly Income)	

▭ Chapter 4 Word Bank

Word or term	Sentence or phrase and page	Meaning	My mastery level of the word or term		
			I understand its meaning.	I can use it in a sentence.	I can spell it correctly.
advice	a piece of advice Some advice Lots of advice				
mind map					
graphic organizer					
dilemma					
case study					
pros/cons					
time line					
life list					
financial adviser					

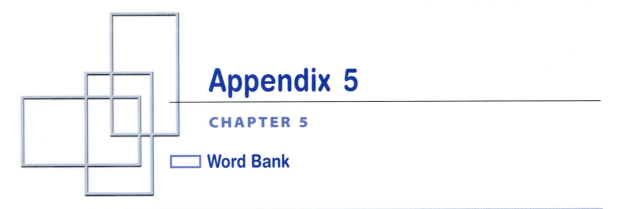

Appendix 5

CHAPTER 5

Word Bank

Word or term	Sentence or phrase and page	Meaning	My mastery level of the word or term		
			I understand its meaning.	I can use it in a sentence.	I can spell it correctly.
etiquette					
jargon					
computer literate					
on task					
brainstorm					
version					
context					

☐ Peer Review Form 5-1 for Group Paragraph

Names of Group Members Who Wrote the Paragraph: _____

_____

Names of Peer Reviewers: _____

_____

Criteria	Yes	No
1. Is there a clear topic sentence that tells which technology is the subject of the writing?		
2. Does the paragraph have a hook?		
3. Are there three major points that explain or support the topic sentence?		
4. Are there enough details or examples for each major point?		
5. Does the concluding sentence make the paragraph more interesting?		
6. Do you notice any grammar, punctuation, or spelling errors? If yes, put a check mark in the margin of the line where you found the problem.		
7. What is one thing about the paragraph that you liked? Be specific.		
8. Make one specific suggestion for improving the paragraph.		

▭ Peer Review Form 5-2

Writer's Name: _____

Peer Reviewer's Name: _____

1. How many paragraphs are there? Circle the answer.	1 2 3 paragraphs	
Criteria	**Yes**	**No**
2. Does each paragraph have a topic sentence?		
3. Are there three reasons for choosing the technology?		
4. Are there enough examples or details to explain the topic sentence(s)?		
5. Does each paragraph have a concluding sentence?		
6. Did you notice any grammar, punctuation, or spelling mistakes? If so, make a check mark in the margin near the mistake.		
7. What did you like best about the paragraph(s)?		
8. What is your favorite sentence in the writing? Why do you like it?		

Index